The Power of Silence

LANGUAGE AND LANGUAGE BEHAVIORS SERIES

Howard Giles

SERIES EDITOR

Department of Communication
University of California, Santa Barbara

This series is unique in its sociopsychological orientation to "language and language behaviors" and their communicative and miscommunicative consequences. Books in the series not only examine how biological, cognitive, emotional, and societal forces shape the use of language, but the ways in which language behaviors can create and continually revise understandings of our bodily states, the situations in which we find ourselves, and our identities within the social groups and events around us. Methodologically and ideologically eclectic, the edited and authored volumes are written to be accessible for advanced students in the social, linguistic, and communication sciences as well as to serve as valuable resources for seasoned researchers in these fields.

Volumes in this series

1. THE POWER OF SILENCE: *Social and Pragmatic Perspectives*
   Adam Jaworski
2. AFRICAN AMERICAN COMMUNICATION: *Ethnic Identity and Cultural Interpretation*
   Michael L. Hecht, Mary Jane Collier, and Sidney A. Ribeau

Volumes previously published by Multilingual Matters in the series Monographs in the Social Psychology of Language and in the series Intercommunication may be obtained through Multilingual at 8A Hill Road, Clevedon, Avon BS21 7 HH, England.

Editorial Advisory Board

The Power of Silence

Social and Pragmatic Perspectives

ADAM JAWORSKI

LANGUAGE AND LANGUAGE BEHAVIORS
volume 1

SAGE Publications
International Educational and Professional Publisher
Newbury Park London New Delhi

For information address:

SAGE Publications, Inc.
2455 Teller Road
Newbury Park, California 91320

SAGE Publications Ltd.
6 Bonhill Street
London EC2A 4PU
United Kingdom

SAGE Publications India Pvt. Ltd.
M-32 Market
Greater Kailash I
New Delhi 110 048 India

Printed in the United States of America

Library of Congress Cataloging-in-Publication Data

Jaworski, Adam, 1957-
The power of silence: social and pragmatic perspectives / Adam Jaworski.
p. cm.—(language and language behaviors : v. 1)
Includes bibliographical references and index.
ISBN 0-8039-4966-9.—ISBN 0-8039-4967-7 (pbk.)
1. Silence. 2. Communication. 3. Pragmatics. I. Title.
II. Series.
P95.53.J38 1993
302.2—dc20 92-30571

93 94 95 96 10 9 8 7 6 5 4 3 2 1

Sage Production Editor: Astrid Virding

For Ania

Contents

Preface xi

1. Silence and the Study of Communication 1
2. Silence and Speech 28
3. The Pragmatics of Silence 66
4. The Politics of Silence and the Silence of Politics 98
5. The Extensions of Silence 140
6. Conclusion 166

References 171

Index 185

About the Author 191

Preface

This book deals with silence in many ways. It is meant to be a theoretical account of different communicative aspects of silence. I am not claiming to have covered the subject comprehensively. However, a wide range of communicative situations—linguistic and nonlinguistic—will be referred to, which will allow me to form generalizations. This is also a functional not a structural study of silence, that is, I am more interested in how it works rather than what it is (see Chapter 2).

On several occasions I depart from the rigid confines of linguistics and investigate silence in areas other than linguistic communication. However, I remain consistent in applying the same frameworks of analysis for the study of linguistic and nonlinguistic silences. In this way I want to contribute to the integrative study of culture, of which language study forms just a part. In other words, I believe that cultural systems are, to a great extent, communicative systems and that language is only one, although probably the most important, of the communicative (sub)systems. Analyzing linguistic phenomena such as silence in association with related aspects of other cultural-communicative systems opens new ways of studying socially motivated language use in general and of silence in particular.

As a starting point, in Chapter 1, an overview of research on silence is offered. It covers a large body of research that has had the most decisive role in shaping my own ideas on silence. Chapter 2 begins with the presentation of my philosophical-methodological position, which determines my approach to the object of this study. Then speech and silence are contrasted and compared.

In the course of juxtaposing both categories, I identify and suggest those characteristics of silence that, to me, are the most important from the communicative point of view. The description of the relevant features of silence does not constitute an end in itself. On the contrary, it is geared toward the rejection of any "final" definition of silence, and it is subordinate to the theories used in the later chapters. Chapter 3 discusses the pragmatic aspects of communicating with silence. It is argued, for example, that in theoretical pragmatic terms silence can be accounted for by the same principles as speech. The most important applied section of the book is contained in Chapter 4, where I present the role that silence plays in politics. There silence is discussed in terms of control, manipulation, and oppression of others. Finally, Chapter 5 diverges from linguistics more significantly than in any other part of the book, and it is claimed that silence may be viewed not only as a linguistic or communicative category present in interpersonal, social, and political discourse but also as a mode of expression in the arts. I also argue that the concept of acoustic silence can be extended to the visual media.

In writing this book I have used several theoretical frameworks. The major ones are the following: Brown and Levinson's theory of politeness, Leach's theory of taboo, Rosch's prototype theory, Sperber and Wilson's relevance theory, and Goffman's frame analysis. Other influences will also become quite obvious. This means that my approach is intentionally eclectic and that I am not suggesting a single theory of silence. Instead, I want to show silence as a rich and powerful tool of communication and to provide some clues as to how it works in different areas of human communication and how it can be accounted for by various theories. One of the outcomes of this approach in the positivistic tenor of the book is the sense that I am explicitly arguing throughout the following pages for the recognition of silence as a legitimate part of the communicative system comparable with speech. I am not denying that in many situations silence can be communicatively empty, but these instances of silence will not be of much concern here.

Most of the research for this volume was carried out during my stay at the American University in Washington, D.C., during the academic year 1987-1988. I would like to express my deep gratitude to Professor Jacek Fisiak, director of the School of English at

Adam Mickiewicz University in Poznán, for enabling me to do my work there as well as for his support for this project and giving me formal assistance when I came back with the unfinished manuscript to Poznán. I am equally grateful to Professor Karol Janicki for his enthusiasm, encouragement, and friendship. Karol's own work and the long conversations we have had in the past few years have shaped my philosophical approach to the study of language. I would like to acknowledge his influence, which is also very visible in this book.

In the initial stages of collecting materials for this book I spent a useful month in London in June 1987. This stay was supported by a generous grant from the British Council and I would like to thank the then English Language Officer in the British Council office in Warsaw, Mr. Roger Woodham, for his support and assistance. When in London, I benefited from the discussion of relevance theory with Dr. Deirdre Wilson. Special thanks are due to Alison Piper for providing me with accommodations in her lovely cottage; a memorable visit to the Tate Gallery; and all the discussions we had on language, art, and silence.

I would like to thank my friend and colleague from Lodz University Dr. Ala Kwiatkowska for several useful references and cheerful correspondence.

Several people have read parts or the entire typescript of the book in various draft forms and offered helpful comments. I would particularly like to thank Professors Muriel Saville-Troike, Nikolas Coupland, Ruta Nagucka, Kari Sajavaara, Karol Janicki, Cheris Kramarae, Peter Trudgill, Laura Klos-Sokol, and Wlodzimerz Sobkowiak.

I have greatly profited from the advice and helpfulness of the series editor Professor Howard Giles. His detailed comments on the final draft of this volume were invaluable; so was his patience when I spent too much time working on the revisions.

Many thanks are due to the World Association for Christian Communication for providing me with the 1982 issue of their journal *Media Development* devoted to silence in communication.

The book took its final shape during my stay at the Department of Applied Linguistics at Birkbeck College, University of London, in 1991-1992. My sincere thanks go to everybody at the department there for providing me with a friendly atmosphere and excellent working conditions.

I would like to thank Ewa Jaworska-Borsley and J. R. Thomas for their comments on the matters of style, my friend Andrzej Wilczak for being the source of unfailing support when I needed it most during my stay in Washington, D.C., and Mum and Dad for being Mum and Dad.

Last but not least, thanks to Ania and Maja for their continuing love, support, and friendship.

None of these individuals is to be held responsible for the ideas put forward here and the obscurities that remain.

CHAPTER ONE

Silence and the Study of Communication

1.1 Introduction

It is common in linguistics writings to place one's object of study in relation to all the branches of the discipline and to specify the one it most appropriately belongs to. Silence, however, cannot be confined to only one branch of linguistics. It cuts across different levels of linguistic usage bearing relevance to the social, political, and emotional aspects governing the lives of individuals and whole communities (Saville-Troike, in press). I am not claiming that silence is central to all study of language, but it can be said to have an important position in those branches of linguistics that deal with how people actually communicate with each other.[1] Therefore, the main task of this chapter is to place silence in the study of *communication*.

1.2 The Problem of Problems

As will be made clearer in §2.2, I believe in linguistic research geared toward the solution of problems: practical or theoretical but not trivial or pseudoproblems (cf. Janicki, 1990; Öhman, 1989). An important practical problem that is worth examining by linguists is that of miscommunication on every possible level of interaction, for example, interpersonal, intergroup, or intercultural.

The importance of the study and understanding of silence has been demonstrated in two popular books by professional linguists (Tannen, 1986; Scollon & Scollon, 1987). They have addressed the questions of miscommunication (Tannen) and what Scollon and Scollon call *responsive* communication. The tenor of the books is popular (much needed indeed), but their implications are relevant to all students of communication.

The central question for both books is Why do native speakers of the same language sometimes not understand each other in a conversation? The *same language* means English here, but the issue of miscommunication and much of its explanation (largely in line with the universal politeness theory of Brown and Levinson, 1978/1987) could probably be extended over all the languages. Tannen seeks to explain this problem by resorting to the notion of different conversational styles.[2] It turns out in Tannen's work that the speaker's conversational style carries as much (if not more) meaning as the sum total of the dictionary definitions of the words in his or her utterance.

When talking to someone, you can be direct or indirect about something, you can be polite by showing involvement or deference, you can use many or just a few words to express the same idea. All of these general strategies of communication have certain advantages. Directness is less ambiguous than indirectness. Indirectness allows the other person to choose the interpretation of your utterance that suits him or her best. Involvement shows your fondness for the other person, while deference shows respect. A longer utterance is usually associated with greater politeness, while communicating an idea in just a few words can be very economical. Apart from the payoffs, however, there are traps in all of these tactics as well. Generally speaking, directness, involvement, and brevity may be interpreted as leaving the listener with no choices, an imposition on him or her, and superficiality, respectively. On the other hand, indirectness, deference, and elaborate utterances can make the listener feel that the speaker is insincere, indifferent, and evasive, respectively.

This book is not intended as an instruction manual. It does not offer any recipes for avoiding conflict or how to communicate with others successfully. However, the importance of identifying and solving various communicative problems will be present throughout, as an underlying, regulative idea for the plan of the book.

1.3 Silence and (Mis)Communication

The awareness of the fact that *how* we say something means at least as much as *what* we say is the central underlying idea of the books by Tannen (1986), and Scollon and Scollon (1987). The authors make their readers aware of the possible and actual miscommunication problems as well as advise them on how to handle situations particularly threatening to their relationships with others.

1.3.1 Communication

But what does silence have to do with that? Why should not saying anything be significantly related to speaking? In my view, the main common link between speech and silence is that the same interpretive processes apply to someone's remaining meaningfully silent in discourse as to their speaking. Consider the following example from Polish.

Shortly after the wedding of her daughter, our next-door neighbor visited my wife and me. In order to hear what the purpose of her visit was my wife and I invited her to sit down in the living room and we started chatting. At one point the neighbor turned to me and asked me how much she owed me for a small favor I had done for her in connection with the wedding. I was genuinely appalled at the question so I *did not say anything* and just looked peeved at the woman. After a moment, she said, slightly embarrassed, *"Czy mam wyskoczyc przez okno?"* ("Do you want me to jump out of the window?"). I said, *"Tak"* ("Yes"). Then we changed the topic, and after feeding us some fresh neighborly gossip, she left.

This example clearly illustrates how silence can carry meaning. I did not reply verbally to her question about the money, but she knew that I was offended by her inquiry, and she also realized that I was not going to accept any form of payment for the favor (which would have then turned into a service). I knew she did not intend to be rude to me, but I felt insulted. If I had decided to tell her that

I thought she was being rude to me at that moment, I may have hurt her in turn. By not saying anything, I simply allowed her to come up with the most relevant interpretation of my silence and then, because of my indirectness, she was able to turn the situation into a joke, which I accepted.

Or take another Polish example. The scene is a small bathroom and the time is early morning before going to work. The husband is shaving and the wife enters to blow dry her hair.

Wife: Przeszkadzam ci? ("Am I disturbing you?")
Husband: [silence]
Wife: [silence, walks out]

In this example, the wife interpreted her husband's silence as a yes. He interpreted her silence as "Okay, I'll come back when you're done." Their exchange was economical, efficient, and to the point.

Our ability to use silence appropriately in our own speech and the adequate interpretation of the silences of others are indispensable for successful communication. Therefore, I believe children acquire the ability to use and understand silence very much in the same manner that they acquire all the other linguistic skills in the acquisition process.[3]

1.3.2 Miscommunication

Of course, things do not always go so smoothly as in the "neighbor" and "bathroom" examples. Silence can cause trouble, too. Many teachers should find the following example a familiar one. (The teacher and the students are Polish, but the class is taught in English.) A group of undergraduate students is asked a question of opinion about a theoretical point they have been discussing for some time.

Teacher: So, what do you think of X?
Students: [silence, looking down]
Teacher: Fine. . . . Sure. . . . Yeah, I agree. . . . That's a good point you've made. . . .

Students: [giggle]

The teacher's interpretation of the students' silence is open to several possibilities. For example, the silence may signal the students' lack of relevant knowledge to answer the question ("You have not taught us enough about the problem you're asking."), it may indicate their hostility toward the teacher and an uncooperative attitude ("We do not like you and we are not going to talk to you."), or it may mark the students' shyness ("We are afraid of saying something stupid."). Regardless of the accurate interpretation of the ensuing silence, the joking behavior of the teacher (quite successful, judging by the giggling that followed it) functioned as relief for the tension created by the awkward silence. (Note that in the "neighbor" example joking was also used as a strategy to alleviate the effect of silence.)

Another classroom example, this time from a Polish elementary-school setting, illustrates how one instance of silence is differently interpreted by two individuals. The teacher asks one pupil to express his opinion on the poem that has been read in class. The boy stands up and remains silent. The teacher interprets his silence as an inability to formulate any opinion on the poem, says nothing to the boy, and asks another one to complete the task. The next boy stands up and says: "I am of the same opinion as my friend." General laughter follows, but it can be safely assumed that the latter boy interpreted the silence of the former as an expression of a negative opinion about the poem.

However, in many cases silence affects human lives more profoundly in a negative way, and mere joking is not a sufficient remedy for the resulting tension. Some people, for example, have the habit of keeping silent more than they are expected to. The so-called strong, silent man is a case in point (Tannen, 1986). His silence may seem quite attractive on stage in the portrayal of fictitious characters or at the beginning of a relationship between a man and a woman, but a woman confronted with a man's silence in a long-term relationship often finds it "like a brick wall against which she is banging her head" (Tannen, 1986, p. 116). See also §4.4.6 for a brief discussion of other aspects of male silence.

1.3.3 Pausing

Misjudging someone's use of silence can take place in many contexts and on many levels. Take pausing, for example. One's conversational style may be marked by frequent pausing, thus giving room (or time) for the discourse partner to jump into the conversation by taking his or her next turn. Some speakers, however, may think that the pauses others leave for them are not long enough to claim the floor without being rude, while it may be the feeling of the other party that longer pauses would create awkward silences. Such differences in the perception and valuation of pauses may lead to conflict. The person who does not tolerate long pauses may wonder why the other does not want to talk, whereas the person who needs longer pauses to take a turn may think of his or her interlocutor as intolerably talkative. Says Tannen (1986):

> Such differences are not a matter of some people expecting long pauses and others expecting short ones. Long and short are relative; they have meaning only in comparison to something—what's expected, or someone else's pause. Someone who expects a shorter pause than the person she's speaking to will often start talking before the other has a chance to finish or to start. Someone who is waiting for a longer pause than the person she's speaking to won't be able to get a word in edgewise. (p. 29)

Fighting for the floor can be quite frustrating especially, in a culture that values more talk and faster talk over less talk and slower talk. Anglo-American culture, and probably most Western cultures, subscribe to such evaluative stereotypes (Scollon, 1985). Therefore, we accelerate our conversations with others and avoid pauses at all cost, because we think that whatever silences occur in discourse they inevitably indicate lack of mutual rapport between the interlocutors.

Cultural attitudes to discourse silence and tempo of speech are very important in assessing the perceived success of speakers in getting their point across. When Lech Walesa and Tadeusz Mazowiecki were running for president of Poland, a press article compared the success and effectiveness of their respective campaigns. Among other things, the author of the article contrasted Walesa's and Mazowiecki's discourse styles. Walesa's style—

marked by fast tempo, varied intonation, and absence of pauses—was evaluated more positively (as more effective) than Mazowiecki's style—described as monotonous and marked by long silences:

> Walesa raises his voice, shouts, suddenly slows down, laughs and pulls a face. He does not hesitate for a second, and even interrupts questions which are too long, while sometimes says frankly to somebody from his entourage "I'm lost." There are no longueurs. . . .
> If only the prime minister [Mazowiecki] knew that he should speak to the microphone and to the people, not to himself! He talks quietly, slowly, monotonously, with multisecond pauses. (Leski, 1990, p. 3)[4]

The above example shows that in political discourse, fast speech, loudness, and constant shifting between different speech styles are more highly valued than speaking slowly, quietly, and monotonously. As will be further demonstrated in Chapter 4, this cultural valuation of noise over silence is effectively used by politicians appearing in the media for two purposes. One is when they have nothing relevant to say and the other is when they want to conceal something. In cases like this, the effect is excessive verbiage or gibberish. It may be devoid of any content on the semantic level but gives wide audiences an impression that the communicator is either very knowledgeable or in control of the situation or information or that he or she has all these qualities. The fact that the message may not be at all clear is irrelevant.

1.4 Facilitative Uses of Silence

The last section ended with an example of the general Western bias in favor of speech rather than silence. This is not to say, however, that silence is not at all recognized as a possible means of communication or that it is unable to perform important communicative functions. This section explicitly deals with the facilitative uses of silence, just as the *positivity theme* of silence is more or less directly present throughout the whole book.

In Chapter 5, where silence is linked with other, nonacoustic means of communication, it will be noted that silence requires high participation involvement and a lot of filling in of information to be fully understood and interpreted. In Sperber and Wilson's (1986) terms (see §3.5.2), the processing effort necessary for the interpretation of silence is greater than in the case of most forms of speech. However, silence, together with other forms of indirect communication, has certain advantages for communicators, for example, in strengthening their confidence in the closeness of their relationship or in going beyond the limits of words to deal with the unspeakable in psychologically extreme states. This use of silence is commonly exploited in literature, where, according to Hassan (1971, p. 13, 1967), the inability of words to express such extreme mental states such as the "void, madness, outrage, ecstasy, [and] mystic trance" occurs.

As will be mentioned later (§2.6.1), speech can often act as a deterrent to and terminator of communication. For example, when leave-taking routines are exchanged there is nothing more that can be said. Formally, then, the meeting or relationship is over. This is why the relatives of terminally ill patients do not usually use words to say the final good-bye to their loved ones (Lynch, 1977). Silence leaves them an out to come back to the relationship in case a miracle happens.

This is not to say that silence is an adequate medium of communication only in extreme situations, involving matters of life and death, as in the preceding example. Silences occur and mean something all the time. Some instances of silence are more easily recognized and identified than others that appear concealed in a multitude of words.

1.4.1 Silence in Face-to-Face Interaction

In their responsive communication manual, Scollon and Scollon (1987) advise their readers to adopt these negatively stereotyped communicative strategies: pausing, slowing down, waiting for the other party to resume speaking after he or she has stopped talking, waiting to speak last, and giving slow answers. Some of the reasons for advocating such behavior are the following: pausing before giving an answer to a question gives the other person some room to speak some more, giving others more time to present their case will make them more comfortable and will improve their exposition, hesitating in one's response gives necessary time to formulate the main or final point as well as allowing one to analyze the other person's arguments more carefully, waiting to speak last allows you not to impose your own topic on others and not to give the impression of trying to dominate the others. The Scollons plead for relaxed schedules and working on *flexitime.* Communicators should not avoid uncomfortable moments in conversation, but should learn to be comfortable with them and use them to find the really important points in conversation. Thus, in case of miscommunication, instead of covering up the possible lack of synchronizing between each other by more uncomfortable talk, interlocutors should take their time and refrain from speaking to restore the lost balance.

Despite our possible skepticism about the feasibility and usefulness of such communicative prescriptions, Scollon and Scollon argue convincingly for *slower* communication. Consider, for example, the revealing fact that some channels of communication, by their nature, prevent us from responding to the other party immediately after receiving a message. Scollon and Scollon (1987) present this point in a section of their book titled "Two-Way Communication":

> Communication involves both sending and receiving. The more feedback there is, the more effective. The important thing is how quickly you get the feedback. When you publish a book it may be years between the time you write and the time you get a response from the audience. When you begin an advertising campaign it may be weeks or months between beginning and feedback. In a personal letter the feedback may take from days to weeks. A computer conference may give you feedback within from minutes to days. Face-to-face communication gives you immediate feedback. As you talk you are reading the response of the person you are talking to.
>
> In ANY form of communication it is important to understand what is a reasonable amount of time for people to take to respond. The most common error is taking action before a reasonable amount of time for the response has passed. Always allow extra time for people to respond to your messages.

> **RECOMMENDATION:** In any medium wait longer to respond than you originally have planned. (p. 36).

The work by Scollon and Scollon suggests that to improve the quality of communication with others in a fast and noisy culture it pays to pause, keep silent, and slow down.[5]

1.4.2 Silence in the Classroom

The enhancing role of increased silent periods for communication has also been well documented by Rowe (1974) in her study of the influence of pausing on the quality of instruction in the classroom. Rowe studied two types of *wait-time:* (1) the teacher's pause between the end of his or her question and the beginning of the student's response and (2) the teacher's pause between the end of the student's response and the teacher's beginning of his or her response to it, next question, and so on. Rowe's extensive recordings of classroom interaction (in elementary-school science programs in the United States) showed the average length of teachers' wait-time of type 1 to be 1 second, and of type 2 to be 0.9 seconds. Having trained teachers to increase both types of wait-time from an average of about one second to an average of three seconds the following variables changed their values:

1. The length of student response increased from a mean of seven words to a mean of 27 words.
2. The mean number of appropriate unsolicited responses increased from five to 17.
3. Mean failure to respond drops from seven to one.
4. Mean incidence of evidence-inference statements increases from six to 14.
5. Average incidence of soliciting, structuring, and reacting moves increases from five to 32.
6. Number of speculative responses increases from a mean of two to a mean of seven.
7. Incidence of student-student comparisons of data increases.
8. Frequency of student-initiated questions increases from a mean of one to a mean of four. (Rowe, 1974, pp. 221-222)

It is not difficult to observe that in the Rowe study slowing down the rate of speech and pausing more than usual improved the quality of classroom interaction, which is just what Scollon and Scollon (1987) suggested would happen for communication processes in general. Besides, Rowe (1974) states that the increase of the amount of wait-time indicates that teachers' expectations toward the performance of weak students improve.

1.5 Other Positive Reactions to Silence

This is not to say that the Scollons or Rowe were the first, or exceptional, Westerners to advance the idea of the benefits of slower and quieter communication. The positive value of silence in conversation has been recognized by various authors from the same cultural background. For example, making use of silence has been advised to married couples (O'Neill & O'Neill, 1972) and to managers in speaking to their subordinates (Farr, 1962). Cook (1964) has observed that silence is characteristic of successful psychotherapeutic interviews, whereas a lack of silence characterizes unsuccessful cases. Johannesen (1974) mentions the general semanticists' (e.g., Barbara, 1958; Korzybski, 1933) idea that healthy communication requires an accurate understanding of silence. Outside of linguistics or communicative literature, Rooney (1987) makes a plea for more silence in general and for the acceptance and tolerance of only those noises that are either natural (e.g., thunder and the bellowing of a volcano) or justified (e.g., the sound of the lawn mower working next door).[6]

By summarizing Tannen's, the Scollons', and Rowe's applied work on silence and pausing as well as by putting it in a slightly wider context, I hope to have shown the general relevance of this book's subject—silence—to an understanding of human communication. It is also my conviction that the study of silence in communication can easily go beyond the level of face-to-face interaction (see Chapters 4 and 5). As the references to this book show, a large body of research on various theoretical and practical

aspects of pausing and silence already exists. It cuts across various levels of language study and also goes beyond linguistics. I would like to turn to some of this research now and, without any claims to being comprehensive, outline its focal points.

1.6 Selective Summary of Research on Silence

Having outlined the contrasts between the positive-facilitative versus the negative-inhibitive approach to communicative silence, it is time to present different levels of linguistic analysis at which silence has been studied. One major theoretical implication following from this overview is that silence is a possible or actual object of investigation in most well-established fields of linguistics. This places silence in an important position vis-à-vis other components of the linguistic universe.

1.6.1 Silence as Contrast to Speech and Psycholinguistics

The simplest, although not uncontroversial, function of silence one can think of is providing background to speech. Bruneau (1973) offers the analogy of the printed page: "Silence is to speech as the white of this paper is to this print" (p. 18) (although it has to be admitted that Bruneau's study of silence goes a lot deeper than this). Others voice similar definitions of silence as "the contrastive material against which auditory images are cast" (Bowers, Metts, & Duncanson, 1985, p. 523). Of course, few theoretical models would allow for silence to be reduced merely to that: background to speech.

Silence is an important factor in defining the boundaries of utterance, but not all linguists agree that identification of single utterances relies solely on silences in which these stretches of talk are embedded. Schiffrin (1987) discusses different approaches to defining speech units and quotes Harris (1931), who defines an utterance as "any stretch of talk by one person, before and after which there is silence on the part of that person" (pp. 33-34). Others, however, have defined units of speech relying on prosodic features (Boomer, 1965; Lieberman, 1967; Pike, 1945), and still others have combined the criterion of *internal prosody* of the unit with the observation that the tone unit usually follows a pause (Chafe, 1977) or that pauses often follow such units (Brown & Yule, 1983).

Researchers have also differed in their classification of *short* and *long* pauses, setting varying criteria for accepting a pause as a boundary marker. Some find silences of one second or more as sufficiently distinguishable from shorter pauses performing non-boundary functions, whereas others have only studied silences of two seconds or more as boundary pauses (Feldstein & Welkowitz, 1987, pp. 482-483).

Many psycholinguists go beyond the classification of silence as prosodic only. Researchers have observed that the distribution of hesitation phenomena such as filled and unfilled pauses, repeats, and false starts in speech is not random (Maclay & Osgood, 1959) and have claimed that unfilled pauses in speech have cognitive functions as well. In a brief critical summary of the relevant research, Beattie and Bradbury (1979) state that unfilled pauses have been identified to play a prominent role in "lexical selection, holistic planning of phonemic clauses, and suprasentential ideational planning" (p. 226).

Beattie and Bradbury (1979) reject, however, the hypotheses that refer to unfilled pauses as universally cognitive (e.g., Goldman-Eisler, 1967, p. 122). They demonstrate that it is possible to decrease the number and length of unfilled pauses in one's speech without distorting the speech content. This suggests that some unfilled pauses are noncognitive and are not necessary to speech. When Beattie and Bradbury trained speakers to eliminate unfilled pauses from their talk, however, they noticed that the overall speech rate did not change and that other forms of *filled* hesitation increased. This suggests, in turn, that the amount of hesitation necessary for the cognitive processing of speech production is fixed.

In his psychosociolinguistic approach to the study of the well-known *pear-stories*, Chafe (1985) observed that in narratives speakers typically use longer silent pauses to mark the change of the conceptual focus of their stories. When they pause, speakers think of what to say next. Silent pauses, together with filled pauses and expressions like *well, let's see, all right,* and so on, help the speakers buy time to start the narrative and then to move from one focal point of narration to another.

Making a decision as to how to say something is also connected with silent hesitation. Longer silences commonly precede words and expressions that are *low in codability.* On the other hand, there is little or no hesitation before terms that are *high in codability.* For example, in Chafe's (1985) data, no speaker describing a boy riding a bicycle hesitated before saying *bike* or *bicycle* (both words are high in codability). Most speakers, however, paused and hesitated a lot before saying *paddleball* (a word low in codability), when reference to an object thus called was in order.

It follows from the above that pausing belongs to the prosodic, or more generally, paralinguistic system of language. It plays a role in identifying speech units and in making sense out of them. Thus it would be an oversimplification to treat silence *only* as background to speech, and probably no student of communication would claim this to be the sole or main function of silence in language. Rather, as is common in psycholinguistic research, silence in the form of pauses and hesitations is treated on a par with other paralinguistic accompaniments of speech such as voice volume, tempo, pitch, and intensity (Smith, 1984, p. 181).

Psycholinguists have often dealt with the correlation of silent (and nonsilent) pauses with various extralinguistic variables such as personal and social characteristics of the speakers. A summary of relevant research has been provided by Crown and Feldstein (1985). The authors observe, for example, that in studies of speech tempo, extroverts have been found to talk faster than introverts. Moreover, the duration of pauses depends as much on the characteristics of the speaker as on those of the listener. Longer pauses are usually produced by individuals described as "distrustful, easily upset, worrying, shy, suspicious, troubled, fussy, and driven, but also self-sufficient and resourceful" (Crown & Feldstein, 1985, p. 38). Longer pauses are also elicited by listeners who are "precise, skeptical, self-reliant, unsentimental, and practical, but also somewhat careless about social rules" (p. 38). Overall, as has already been said (§1.3.3) in Western culture fast talk, short pauses, and eliciting short speaking turns are viewed more positively than speaking slowly, making long pauses, and allowing the conversational partner to take long speaking turns. Crown and Feldstein note that subjects in their experiments assess speakers who have relatively longer switching pauses in negative terms such as *aloof, rigid, prone to sulk, indolent, self-indulgent,* and *undependable.* The process is, in a sense, reversible—i.e., speaking to socially unattractive partners who are perceived as reserved, restrained, detached, taciturn, sober, timid, and so forth leads to the use of longer turns than when the conversational partner is viewed positively as warmhearted, participating, talkative, cheerful, adventurous, and socially bold (Crown & Feldstein, 1985, p. 39).[7]

A different set of variables has been correlated with pauses by Duez (1982). Among other things, she has examined the differences in the length and distribution of (silent and nonsilent) pauses in three speech styles: political speeches, political interviews, and casual interviews. Nonsilent pauses have been found to be characteristic of both interview styles; casual interviews display a higher ratio of filled hesitation than political interviews, probably due to the fewer constraints felt by the interviewees in a casual interview than in a political one. Nonsilent pauses were almost nonexistent in political speeches, which is quite clear in light of the fact that speakers do not improvise their political speeches but prepare for them and learn them well before delivering them. However, political speeches have scored high on silent pauses. Apart from their function of marking the grammatical structure of the utterance, silent pauses also have the stylistic function of emphasizing arguments and ideas, and they are usually employed by more experienced speakers to impress their listeners and elicit applause.

The frequency of occurrence of hesitation phenomena, including false starts, repetitions, filled pauses, unfilled pauses, and so on, has also been correlated with three types of U.S. television narrative programs: documentaries, prime-time dramas, and soap operas (Johnson & Davis, 1979). The results show a higher incidence of filled and unfilled pauses in familial conversations in soap operas than in the other two formats. The authors have also isolated three conversation styles present in the analyzed segments of the television programs: casual, personal, and intimate. The three styles have been found to influence the hesitation rate in the speech of the characters, although here the results are not as clear-cut. However, in regard to the unfilled pauses, all the television formats showed a greater ratio of unfilled pauses in the intimate style than in the other two.

This section attests to the fact that different forms of pauses (and other hesitation phenomena) occur regularly and that they perform various cognitive, discoursal, and stylistic functions. For example, they are used for planning of utterances, marking boundaries of grammatical clauses, and signaling emphasis. They are formal indicators of particular discourse types and conversational styles.

What seems worth emphasizing once again is that psycholinguistic silence, as its other types, is an axiologically highly charged concept. The strong evaluative feelings associated with silence are both positive and negative. They concern the cultural notions of what makes *good communication* and the social notions of how to be a *successful communicator*. As it happens, this axiological dialectics of silence operates in a system of values that is regarded as universally applicable and natural. It is based on a two-valued system of binary oppositions: plus versus minus, good versus bad, black versus white, and so forth. A lot of material in later chapters is preoccupied with the theoretical and practical consequences of this type of dialectic. In Chapter 2, for example, the absolutist approach to speech as the positive quality and silence as the negative one is refuted. In Chapter 5, different forms of artistic expression are discussed and identified as forms of acoustic silence extended to the visual medium. Using examples from abstract painting, the validity of the positive-negative dichotomy in the assessment of communicative silence will be questioned once again. This will be contrasted with the subjectivity of human experience and interpretation coupled with the prototypical (i.e., nondiscrete or fuzzy) nature of the concept of silence.

1.6.2 Pauses at Turn-Taking Junctures: The Conversational Analysis Approach

Conversational analysts[8] have observed that there is very little overlap in the speech of two or more participants and that the silences occurring between participants' turns tend to be minimal, averaging a few microseconds. However, when silence, defined as the absence of vocalization, does occur at a turn-taking juncture in interaction it can predictably be assigned to one of the following categories:

1. A *gap* before the current speaker who terminates his or her turn assigns the next speaker, before another party in the interaction self-selects to be the next speaker, or before the current speaker claims further right to the floor in the conversation.
2. A *lapse* when the current speaker does not nominate the next speaker but stops speaking, when the next speaker nominated by the current speaker fails to claim the floor, or when another party does not self-select to be the next speaker in the interaction and the current speaker does not resume speaking.
3. A selected next speaker's *significant* (or *attributable*) *silence* after the next speaker is nominated by the current speaker who has stopped speaking (Levinson, 1983, based on Sacks, Schegloff, & Jefferson 1974).

1.6.3 The Ethnographic Approach

So far a few linguistic traditions have been mentioned in connection with their views on the role and functions of silence in conversation. In the course of this book it will become apparent to the reader that I have not adopted any single framework in espousing my ideas on silence. However, it will also be plain enough that certain philosophical and linguistic research traditions have been decisive in shaping my views. Some will be more explicitly drawn on than others. The one in which I find the work on silence to be most stimulating and interesting is the broadly defined ethnographic approach. In this framework, the discussion of the status of *silence in communication* gains more theoretical import than in others by adopting the position that silence and speech are two intersecting and equally relevant communicative categories. The field of study known as the *ethnography of communication* (Hymes, 1962, 1974) has been able to adopt this position because it is a synthesizing discipline combining sociological, interactional, symbolic, and philosophical orientations (Saville-Troike, 1982, pp. 1-2). This position leads ethnographers to the integrated study of human communicative behavior, "within which silence serves variously as prime, substitute, and surrogate, as well as frame, cue, and background" (Saville-Troike, 1985, p. 17).

The most general, theoretical distinction for the study of speech and silence was introduced by Philips (1985). She differentiates between "interaction structured through talk" and "interaction structured through silence."[9] I take the latter concept to incorporate all the situations in which the silent, nonverbal, physical, visual, and other signals *override* speech in interpreting the communicative behavior of the participant(s), although speech and other vocal signals may be present and need not be excluded from the interpretation of a given speech situation structured through silence. The following considerations will all implicitly or explicitly fall back on the theoretical implications of the ethnographic research and will rely greatly on Philips's distinction.

Pittenger, Hockett, and Danehy (1960) state rather eloquently that "it only takes one person to produce speech, but it requires the cooperation of all to produce silence" (p. 88). This implies that meaningful silence takes place only between two or more people. This is also implied later in §3.4.4, when communicative silence is described in greater detail. It is said to occur in situations in which the participants are engaged in communication or when one of them assumes that communication is taking place. However, the involvement of two or more people in *silent communion* is necessarily assumed only when the most prototypical cases of communicative silence are considered. In the less prototypical cases of silent communion only one person need be involved, which can be seen as the counterpart to soliloquy in speech.

Let us consider meditation, for example. Symbolically, the role of the other participant sharing the silent interaction may be attributed to a deity, the whole of nature, all of creation, or any other physical or mental construct, depending on one's philosophical or religious orientation. In a sense, the silent meditating person can also be the only intended recipient of the silence he or she produces. On the face of it, particular instances of meditative silence will not be easily distinguishable from the cases in which an individual's refraining from speaking does not carry any meaning. However, one can also think of certain more prototypical cases of meditative silence, such the Trappist monk praying or contemplating in his cell. An example of a definitely less prototypical, but nonetheless fully legitimate, meditative silence is the scenery-invoked contemplation of a lone tourist in the mountains.[10] Take the following account of Szczypiorski's (1989) experience as a good example of such a *revelational* (Jensen, 1973) function of silence.

> Today, during the walk, when I was pretty exhausted, I sat down on the hummock of an easy hill and leaned against a pine trunk. There was some huge silence around. No breeze, no rustling of the branches, no bird. Silence and nothing else. This was very nice. But, unfortunately, there was also myself. And after a while, unusual shouting rose in myself. This shouting probably swirls always, but I don't hear it because I'm busy with many everyday activities, reading, or simply walking. And in silence, which fell when I sat down, I suddenly heard all my inner voices, chattering and furious, as if they were finally able to shout out to me all the latent themes. . . . Very stupid questions. What next? Why did it happen? What is the way out of this? What should be done? What did I need that for? And there is only one answer all the time: I don't know. (pp. 29-30)

This passage suggests that certain forms of silence facilitate the ego's self-awareness and that *framing,* or casting oneself in external silence can be a unique communicative experience. It also illustrates well the distinction between the author's meditation—internal communication structured through silence—with another silent activity devoid of any communicative intent and consequences: walking.

Both activities mentioned above—meditation and walking—can be said to be structured through silence. The difference between them is that in the case of meditation, as with any meaningful silence, we have to assume that some thought processes are involved (Johannesen, 1974). The generality of this characteristic of meaningful silence makes it applicable to a wide range of situations. Indeed, when one looks at the existing body of research on silence, it is evident that this category has been examined in a multitude of domains, linguistic and nonlinguistic ones, and from a variety of perspectives. Several different orientations in the study of silence have been mentioned so far, for example, the psycholinguistic, paralinguistic, and ethnographic. Others have not been any less significant (although not all of these orientations can be fully accepted here). Semiotic, pragmatic, educational, literary, and philosophical studies of silence have made their own contributions to the field.

Within the tradition of semiotic and pragmatic studies, many authors have presented their views on what silence is, what its functions are, and what human activities are affected by it (e.g., Bruneau, 1973, 1985; Dambska, 1975; Jensen, 1973; Johannesen, 1974; Meerloo, 1975; Poyatos, 1981, 1983, chap. 6; Rokoszowa, 1983; Scott, 1972; The Second Foundation, 1981; Verschueren, 1985, chap. 3). Various lists of properties and meanings of silence that are believed to be the most typical have been compiled. Such lists are necessarily open-ended. Therefore, they vary from one study to another in length, and in the intended or stated level of completeness of description.

1.6.4 Silence in Context

A large group of studies have treated the topic of silence by examining it in specific domains and situations. Their hypotheses about the role of silence in particular communicative situations are usually based on the evidence of empirically collected data. An interesting example of this type of research is Tannen's (1985) work on the apparent *lack* of silence and low level of tolerance for silence among New York Jewish speakers in casual conversations.

Among other contexts,[11] silence has been studied as an important component of classroom interaction (§1.4.2.). Gilmore's (1985) study of ritualistic displays of silence, combined with other types of students' and teachers' nonverbal behaviors, provides further insights into the nature of communication in the school setting. The author interprets a range of students' and teachers' uses of silence and correlates them with certain types of the participants' orientation and attitudes in classroom interaction, for example, coupled with specific body movements and facial expressions, the teachers use silence to show disapproval of their students, to scold them, or to try to restore order in the classroom. The clear, silent messages sent by teachers to their students often mean "Pay attention to me" or "What you're doing is unacceptable to me" (Gilmore, 1985, p. 147). The black students' silences, accompanied by nonverbal behavior, signal compliance with or defiance of the teacher's directives or criticisms. The latter type of ritualistic displays of silence (*stylized sulking*) has especially become a highly predictable act of black students' challenging behavior to an authority (the teacher), and a face-saving strategy in front of the student's peers.[12]

Teachers' silence always marks their dominant status over the students'. This is how they get and focus the students' attention, interrupt them, or relieve the moments of tension. Students' silence is subordinate, although it need not be submissive, as in the case of stylized sulking, which is a sign of the students' reluctance to submit to their teachers' authority.

Gilmore's (1985) work centered on the cultural values attached to the manifestations of silence in a black neighborhood elementary school in a U.S. urban setting. Despite the inequality of status between students and teachers, "the uses and meaning of their silences are actually very similar" (Gilmore, 1985, p. 154). The similarity lies in both teachers' and students' uses of silence in situations of negotiating power: exerting and displaying it in the case of teachers; defying and claiming it in the case of students. In either case, great emotional involvement and tension are present.

High levels of anxiety in the classroom are likely to be manifest in silence, regardless of the cultural background of students and the teaching objectives. A study involving a foreign-language situation (Lehtonen, Sajavaara, & Manninen, 1985) found a correlation between the reticence of Finnish speakers of English and their increased anxiety level in speaking English.

Three interesting articles on the role of silence in the teaching process are John (1972), Dumont (1972), and Philips (1972). Actually, these studies are concerned not only with the use of silence in the classroom but also, and foremost, with the cross-cultural differences in the use and valuation of silence between native Americans and Anglo-Americans and with the educational implications of these differences for native schoolchildren. The main concern of the authors is the potential and actual inequality of native American and Anglo-American children at school. The schools attended by native American children are run by Anglo-Americans and follow the curricula developed according to Anglo-American principles, often significantly different from the native ones (but note the publication year of the papers: 1972).

For example, the Anglo-American culture places much value on children's verbal skills, and the teaching process is largely dependent on verbal interaction between the teacher and the students. Navajo children, however, are more visual in their approach to learning about the surrounding world. They depend more on moving freely around in their environment and exploring natural objects by touching them; in outdoor play, for example, gestures and touching are often used among native American children, but words are seldom used. Thus, with the visual and quiet exploration of the world, a lot of native children may be at a disadvantage when the primary mode of learning is the verbal one. This is well documented by the fact that Indian children are underrated in educators' estimation of their cognitive abilities as these are primarily based on verbal testing techniques (John, 1972). Thus, very often, the only alternatives left to the native American students at Anglo-American schools is to speak English, which they feel uncomfortable with, or to remain silent, which is negatively stereotyped by the majority of teachers who are usually white (Dumont, 1972; see also Murphy, 1970).

Cross-cultural differences in the use and valuation of silence have been explored in the following studies: Basso (1972); Bruneau (1973, 1982); Ganguly (1968-1969); Gardner (1966); Giles, Coupland, and Wiemann (1991); Lebra (1987); Lehtonen and Sajavaara (1985); Nwoye (1985); O'Kelly (1982); Philips (1976, 1985); Samarin (1965); Saunders (1985); Scollon (1985); and Wardhaugh (1986, pp. 234-237). Most of the studies in this group take the Western (usually Anglo-American) perspective as the norm (in a nonprescriptive sense) and present various alternative approaches to the use, distribution, and appreciation of silence. Apart from enhancing cross-cultural awareness, these studies also address important theoretical issues. A recent, systematic overview of cross-cultural aspects of silence in communication can be found in Enninger (1983, 1987).

According to Enninger, silence may be *situation specific* (regardless of culture) or *culture specific.* The former is exemplified by a sound technicians' refraining from speaking while recording a symphony. It does not pose any problems for cross-cultural interpretation, because silence here depends on the practical conventions of the event itself. The latter types of silence are subject to cross-cultural misinterpretation. They may lead to interethnic miscommunication and conflict and give rise to negative stereotyping of individuals and even whole communities. Such silences are more likely to yield negative communicative effects than speech, because their interpretation involves not only the inferencing of their semantic meanings but also the identification of the right silences as meaningful ones and the understanding of the sender's motives for remaining silent.

Cross-cultural uses of silence are rooted in the observation of different types of taboo, practical magic, and in varying beliefs as to how much or little talk is necessary in a given situation. Differences in temporal organization of discourse (chronemics) are also of great significance here. Enninger focuses on the differences in the length of silences (*nonphonations*) between speakers' turns, the length of silences within one speaker's turn, and the length of individual turns. He quotes many sources (which will also partially be mentioned in Chapter 2), illustrating many departures from the low tolerance of silence by mainstream European and American cultures.

Among the Amish, for example, interactive silences are much longer than among the majority of white Americans. In one conversation among three adult Amish speakers, Enninger (1987) recorded "no fewer than eleven between-turn gaps and lapses longer than twenty seconds, the longest being fifty-six seconds" (p. 280). There were no signs of communication breakdown in this or other similar situations observed in the Amish culture, which attests to the commonly held view among the Amish, but not among most other (white) American subcultures, that successful interactive events, such as social visits, do not necessarily involve the use of speech. According to Enninger (1985, 1987), these extended gaps and lapses have probably influenced the American mainstream society's view of the Amish as taciturn and uncooperative.

Other cross-cultural differences occur when silence takes over some functions of verbal formulas (§2.6.1). Enninger states that in some cultures, as among the Amish, silence may replace speech even in the seemingly most verbal act of greeting. For example, it is acceptable for an Amish person entering the home of an Amish neighbor not to knock on the door and not to salute the host. After sitting down, the guest may remain silent for a while before starting to talk. Likewise, the Amish observe very strict rules for maintaining group silence in various ritual and ceremonial situations (e.g., church services, baptisms, and marriage ceremonies). By the reduction of the amount of ceremonial talk—reserved to very few high-ranking participants—the community's silence manifests its unity with the absolute (Enninger, 1983). As these examples indicate, "the replacement of a normally expected formula by silence is not in all cultures read as the formal exponent of an act of hostility" (Enninger, 1987, p. 292).

Shifting away from actual interaction, many studies have analyzed silence in literature. Their orientation ranges from that of literary criticism to ethnography of communication.[13] In the latter studies, the text is treated as a source of data for ethnographic analysis. For example, Basso's (1972) hypothesis about the reasons for maintaining silence among the Western Apache Indians has been tested by Bock (1976) for English on the basis of Shakespeare's plays. As in the Basso study, it turns out that in Elizabethan England silence was triggered, among other factors, by the unclear status of the situation and/or of the participants.

Tannen (1990) uses a conversational analysis approach to her study of silences in Pinter's play *Betrayal* and Mattison's short story "Great Wits." Tannen argues that in both works silences function as signals of conflict in social interaction. In *Betrayal*, silence occurs "at the points where potentially explosive information is confronted," and in "Great Wits," "silence prevents conflict from erupting into damaging confrontation" (Tannen, 1990, p. 260). Such studies have great value in corroborating hypotheses about various communicative functions of silence in naturally occurring speech.[14]

1.7 Conclusion

Silence has many faces. As will be shown later, it is probably the most ambiguous of all linguistic forms. It is also ambiguous *axiologically;* it does both good and bad in communication. On the one hand, silence is useful when one wants to be indirect or to be polite by "leaving options" (Lakoff, 1973). Silence gives the hearer time to think of a response to what has been said before, and it can be used as a conflict-avoidance strategy. It is easier to undo silence than it is to undo words. On the other hand, one's failure to say something that is expected in a given moment by the other party can be interpreted as a sign of hostility or dumbness. This negative aspect of the use of silence becomes especially apparent in cross-cultural communication.

The above summary of research on different functions of silence in communication does not claim to be a comprehensive one. Some important issues in the study of silence have not even been mentioned here. Several problems have merely been signaled without developing elaborate arguments leading to their solution. My aim here was only to indicate how complex the study of silence is and to convince the reader that it is a worthwhile object of linguistic investigation.

The feeling with which I began writing this book was that if we know more about silence, we will know more about ourselves. When I was completing the book's first draft, I realized I was unable to offer many answers. The following questions as well as others remain as open to debate as ever: How do we communicate with each other? Do we talk only when we are speaking? How important are marginal communicative phenomena in discovering other people and the world? What are the social implications of viewing silence as a monolith and absolute versus adopting a more relativistic perspective differentiating among many types of silence? Naturally, I have formulated my own hypotheses and opinions, and I hope that this book can, at least, increase our own awareness about communication, including its marginal forms, and that it has the potential of making us more tolerant and successful communicators.

Notes

1. Verschueren (1985) goes even as far as to say that "silence is no doubt the most marginal aspect of linguistic action imaginable" (p. 74).

2. But see also Janicki (1987) and his account of misunderstanding based on the differences between prototypes of particular concepts held by the members of a speech community.

3. To the best of my knowledge, the development of children's ability to interpret and produce meaningful silences in the language acquisition process has been studied very little. Several psycholinguistic studies have looked at pausing/timing phenomena in children. For example, Kowal, O'Connell and Sabin (1975) found that children's narratives speech rate increases with age due to the decrease in the length and frequency of unfilled pauses. The authors claim that the changes in temporal patterning and vocal hesitations in children reflect cognitive and linguistic functions.

In a very interesting paper, Ure (in press) discusses functional aspects of adults' pausing in speaking to children. The author classifies such pauses (as well as certain verbal cues in the structure of discourse, gaze, posture, laughter, etc.) as *letting-in devices*. These are such facilitative uses of language by mature speakers that enable new speakers to take part in the communicative process and acquire new skills and norms shared by the community. For example, while repeating a nursery rhyme to a child an adult pauses in appropriate moments for the child to complete the lines.

Casual observation of my daughter's verbal behavior between the ages 4 and 5 indicates to me that learning how to interpret another person's silences is not an easy task for a child and can be frustrating. For example, when my daughter calls me to tell me something and I do not *verbally* indicate my willingness to listen (even if I look at her and establish eye contact), she will not say what she wants. Then, after a pause of a few seconds, she will summon me again, saying something like, "Daddy, you know what?" and only if I respond by saying something like, "Yes?" will she talk further. This indicates that a child has to learn to distinguish among different silences, for example, the silence of indifference and refusal to engage in discourse from the silence of the other party's concern for her and the acceptance of her invitation to talk.

4. All translations from Polish into English are my own.

5. This is not to say that fast talk is never desirable. Some situations call for warming up the relationship and speaking faster than usual, which often effects one's being judged positively by others (Scollon & Scollon, 1987, p. 28).

6. It should also be mentioned here that speech plays a positive role in enhancing the meaning and interpretation of silence. This thesis finds convincing support in an interesting study of silence among Trappist monks (Jaksa & Stech, 1978). The authors found that the majority of the monks in different Trappist monasteries enjoyed the easing of the strict rule of near total silence to the new one that read: "Brief, oral communication without asking permission is given to everyone" (p. 14). The monks were of the opinion that the freedom to talk to each other gave them much needed human contact with each other and provided a new, better, more effective, and meaningful perspective on silent meditation.

7. This approach has been criticized for its cultural bias by Scollon (1985); see §2.5.3, and consider the advocation of the use of silence in communication by Scollon and Scollon referred to in §1.4.1.

8. See Levinson (1983) for a convenient summary of research.

9. Philips's distinction has been criticized by Gardner (1986) who claims that the concept of interaction structured through silence is confusing and means the same

as "interaction structured in silence by nonverbal means" (p. 509). I do not find this criticism justified, because Philips's approach encompasses a wider range of communicative silences than Gardner's substitute implies. The distinction and terminology seem also to be justified in view of the general theoretical framework adopted by Philips in her paper. However, I will refrain from arguing for the superiority of one concept over the other, because terminological disputes may only bring more confusion and misunderstanding. (See §2.6.1 for further discussion of Philips's concepts and their implication for the study of silence.)

10. The importance of the meditative aspect of silence has been emphasized by numerous authors (see, for example, Cini, 1987; Dambska, 1975; Ganguly, 1968-1969; Jensen, 1973; Kelsey, 1976; Picard, 1948; Scott, 1972).

11. Several studies have focused on the significance and meaning of silence in religious life and ceremonies (e.g., Bauman, 1974, 1983; Hartley, 1982; Jackson, 1974; Jaksa & Stech, 1978; Maltz, 1985; Strelan, 1982), and on religious silence in a more philosophical and speculative perspective (e.g., Foccardi, 1987; Merton, 1979/1982; Mora, 1987; Neher, 1981; Picard, 1948; Steggink, 1982). Walker (1985) and O'Barr (1982) have studied the uses and effects of silence in the courtroom, and Rice (1961) has examined various legal aspects of the right to be silent. Silence in politics has been analyzed in the studies of Brummett (1980), Erickson and Schmidt (1982), and Gunderson (1961). Caute (1986) has provided an account of silence in the workings of political propaganda. The religious silence of the Quakers and the political uses of silence will be dealt with in greater detail in Chapters 2 and 4, respectively.

12. Because the interpretation of stylized sulking and other types of classroom silences relies on the co-occurrence of body movements, changes of facial expression, various physiological reactions (e.g., blushing), and so on, it is useful here to call on Philips's idea of interaction structured through silence. This is not obviously synonymous with nonverbal communication, because body movements and facial expressions also accompany and influence the interpretation of talk.

13. See, for example, Barthes (1953/1967); Bock (1976); Brown (1972); Collier (1984); Hassan (1967, 1971); Mendez (1972, 1978); Rovine (1987); and Tannen (1990).

14. Silence can be contrasted not only with speech but with other noises as well. This obvious statement has found expression in studies dealing with silence in the nonliterary arts, for example in music. Clifton (1976) has examined the role of pauses in classical music. Silence and theater music have been contrasted by Binns (1982). Cage's (1961) famous book on silence parallels his own experiments with the use of silence in music. Steiner (1979/1982) explores the significance of silence in the interpretation of Schoenberg's opera *Moses and Aaron*.

Finally, we can also speak of the *extensions* of silence in the sense in which this concept has been appropriated by the critics of culture as an aesthetic category (Sontag, 1969). In visual and performing arts, abstraction, simplification of form and ambiguity of expression have been found to be analogous to silence in linguistic communication. Chapter 5 is devoted to the discussion of such visual extensions of silence in the arts.

CHAPTER TWO

Silence and Speech

2.1 Introduction

Can I say something without speaking? Can I remain silent when talking? Does absolute silence exist? If it does, is there also absolute speech? These and other questions will be addressed in this and the next chapter. The main concern will be the communicative value of silence, and as such, it will be contrasted with speech, which is unquestionably treated as a primary communicative category, due to its prevalent use in communication, but not due to its superiority resulting from any theoretical premises. If my task here is to contrast speech and silence to discuss the latter as a carrier of communication, I might be expected first to define both terms to make it clear what they mean. However, I will not do that, and suggest instead that in the course of comparing the properties of speech and silence in Chapters 2 and 3, a contrastive conception of silence in relation to speech will be arrived at (§3.4.4).[1] Further discussion will be based on this understanding of silence. This, however, will not in itself be the main aim of this study. No description of silence that is presented here should be treated as an attempt at formulating its extended, ultimate definition. It should rather be taken as an operational definition that will allow me to account for specific types of communicative behavior and to apply different theories to explain them.

2.2 The Nonessentialist Approach

My reluctance to treat definitions too seriously stems from a philosophical orientation in sociolinguistics suggested by Janicki (1989, 1990). Following Popper's (1945, 1972, 1976) antiessentialist (anti-Aristotelian) philosophy of science, Janicki advocates nonessentialist sociolinguistics.[2] After Popper, Janicki rejects the possibility of arriving at the final definitions (essences) of things, objects, words, concepts, and so forth. Hence, he dismisses defining the analytical categories in terms of which theories are formulated as a desirable or valid research goal. If one's aim is to define concepts he or she will never be able to complete this task because terminological disputes are in principle insoluble (we can endlessly argue about the meaning of words) and because they lead to an infinite regress of definitions. For example, when a concept, such as *speech community* or *communicative competence* is defined we can further ask questions about the meanings (definitions) of words (concepts) used in the first definition, and then about the meanings of words used to define the latter, and so on *ad infinitum*.

I will illustrate my point with an example from a paper that can be called *theoretical contrastive pragmatics* (Oleksy, 1984). This paper aspires to formulate the foundations of pragmatic contrastive studies. It takes the speech act as its main unit of description/comparison and sets out to propose "ways by means of which the type of SA [speech act] that the speaker has performed could be defined" (Oleksy, 1984, p. 352). And the author goes on:

> The definition of the type of SA that the speaker has performed will be referred to as the assignment of the Speech Act Value (SAV) to the speaker's utterance.
>
> Suggested below are three possible steps leading to the assignment of the SAV to S's utterance:
>
> i. Illocutionary force (IF) of S's utterance must be defined.
> i. Felicity conditions (FC) for SA which S has performed must be specified [i.e., defined].
> iii. Sociocultural context (SC) in which SA typically occurs must be specified [i.e., defined]. (p. 352)

Then, Oleksy defines the terms IF, FC, and SC, which for him is a necessary step before he can define the type of a speech act that has been performed by a speaker. Take a look at his definition of FC:

> FC's are what the speaker assumes about the addressee, about the content of what is being communicated, and about the empirical setting in which an SA occurs. Judgments concerning felicity of an SA rely heavily on general principles of conversation as well as on the unique conditions for the SA being performed by the speaker at a given time and in a given context. (p. 353)

The effect of the procedure described above can be summarized in the following way:

1 We want to know *the* definition of a given type of speech act.
2. To achieve number 1 we have to find out (define) the speech act value (SAV) of a speech act.
3. To define SAV we need to define IF, FC, and SC.
4. It is quite clear that, given felicity conditions, for example, before we can *really* define them, we first have to define or agree on the meaning of the terms used in their definition, such as *speaker, addressee, empirical setting, general principles of conversation, unique conditions,* and *context.*

This type of essentialist approach leads to what is called here the *infinite regress of definitions* and to futile terminological disputes (*verbalism* in Popper's terminology).[3] Janicki (1990) claims that linguists do seriously engage in terminological disputes, asking "What is" questions, and that they view them as legitimate and soluble research tasks. Consider the following two examples:

> Few problems continue to generate so much endeavor and so much conflict as the problem of style. Even conferences are called to answer the questions: '*What is style?*', 'How can we study it?' . . . Marozean began by admitting that the question of style is as open today as it was two millennia ago. Some progress was made in the nineteenth century when scholars began 'to treat style as an object of scientific inquiry', but consequently the question of *what style is* became more pressing. (Gray quoted in Janicki, 1990, p. 64; emphasis in the original)

> Tanzania's linguistic composition is complex, for there are today over one hundred vernacular language groups. This is, however, a rough estimate, since little analysis has been done as to *what objectively constitutes a dialect, and what a language.* (Zuengler quoted in Janicki, 1990, p. 63, emphasis in the original)

These two, and in fact many other, examples indicate that a lot of linguists believe that linguistic concepts are discrete categories, which can be finally (ultimately, objectively) defined, and that pursuing their definitions is a worthwhile task. This view is totally rejected here. Linguistic concepts, including silence, are viewed in this book as *prototypes* in Rosch's (1978) sense, and thus they are indiscrete categories (they have fuzzy edges). It is impossible to define concepts once and for all because we are always left with some fuzzy cases (the least prototypical members of categories). Therefore, definitions need not be taken very seriously, unless they are meant to be working or operational. As such, they can limit terminological discussions, save time and paper. And, as Dressler (1988) put it in regard to linguistic classifications—and we can extend his idea to include working definitions—they "must have a purpose and must be based on an underlying theory" (p. 1).

What is more important in research is to create theories as well as to identify and solve *problems* (cf. §1.2). Once theories are available, they can be checked against data. When a given theory seems to be the best in accounting and explaining our data, it can be used to solve practical problems (i.e., those that are external to the theory itself) or it can be used to solve further theoretical (e.g., methodological) problems. Linguistics has had a long tradition of working on both types of problems. As far as the practical problems are concerned, some examples are making foreign-language teaching more effective; explaining miscommunication; and identifying and fighting sexism, racism, and totalitarian propaganda. This book addresses various practical problems related to the concept of silence in Chapter 4. Before that, a few theoretical problems are addressed, of which relating data to specific pragmatic and anthropological theories gains the primary importance.

There is not enough time and space here to discuss the nonessentialist approach to sociolinguistics in greater detail (e.g., Janicki, 1990). Suffice it to say that because there is no objective way of drawing dividing lines between linguistic categories, they can only be separated one from another by way of theoretically motivated decisions. Thus all definitions of concepts have to be treated as theoretically (versus objectively) motivated, and their value is no more than operational. Claiming that we *really* know what something is (or that such knowledge is possible in principle) is here called the *essentialist approach*. In my *nonessentialist approach*, I will not make any claims as to what silence *really* is. Consequently, whatever definitions, characterizations, or taxonomies appear in this book, they are meant as operational ones.

In sum, I do not wish to start my analysis of silence and speech with any technical discussion of what speech and silence are. For the most part, I will use both terms, and especially the term *silence*, in their everyday senses, each time making it clear which of their several senses (or extensions) is referred to.[4] It will become evident later that the nonessentialist approach to the study of silence will allow me to include in this study various types of linguistic items that would otherwise have been left out, and that trying to define the object of my study before applying a theoretical framework to its analysis would have had a limiting effect on the development of the argument.

2.3 Essentialism in the Study of Silence: Some Examples

Several studies of silence reveal the nature of the essentialist approach. It is easy to notice the inadequacies resulting from such essentialist thinking about silence. For example, Dauenhauer's (1980) book on silence has a clearly defined task. The author states at the beginning that the main questions he has tried to answer in his work are "What is silence? And what is its ontological significance?" (Dauenhauer, 1980, viii). Trying to answer such questions (i.e., define silence) seems to be a rather unpromising task, although in undertaking it one must assume that there are satisfactory answers. It also implies that one is able to get to the *essence* of things, in this case to the essence of silence.

Indeed, Dauenhauer's book seems to be an example of verbalism brought about by essentialist thinking. Despite its many interesting insights, Dauenhauer's book seems to ramble on in search of the true meaning of silence only to conclude at the end that the book has failed to achieve its primary goal and that it probably can never be achieved. The author seems to be content with his own analysis of silence, but adds that "however fruitful my interpretation may be, no ontological interpretation of silence can be *definitively* established" (Dauenhauer, 1980, p. 176).

There are several authors who seem to believe that the essence of silence can be revealed in establishing its taxonomies, status, or relationship to other concepts. The paper on silence by a duet of linguists calling themselves The Second Foundation (1981) has a section titled "A (Partial) Taxonomy of Silences" (p. 350). Should the reader be led to believe by this that a *complete* taxonomy of silences is possible? Of course, every taxonomy, being a form of description (definition), is partial and no comprehensive (ultimate, final, objective) taxonomy is possible to arrive at. However, Poyatos (1983) would not probably agree. In the chapter devoted to silence and stillness in his book, there is a section titled "The *True* Status of Silence and Stillness in Interaction" (p. 219; emphasis added). Poyatos (1983) also comments that other linguists have rarely "referred to silence as an element of interaction, thereby missing the *true* relationship between language and interaction" (p. 221; emphasis added).

Another essentialist approach to the study of silence is apparent in Ganguly (1968-1969). First, he asserts that the inherent ambiguity of language (i.e., words), is responsible for the impossibility of achieving intended *ideal* or *precise* communication among people. Therefore, people experience great frustration and cannot feel secure and free when they use language, although language promises them both security and freedom. Then Ganguly turns to silence, which he refers to in terms of the Indian yoga tradition of purifying and emptying the mind of verbalism and not simply as the absence of speech. This silence is a kind of absolute, and Ganguly claims that it is only in silence that people can be totally secure and free. Silence is "the limit of our world of description or language" (Ganguly, 1968-1969, p. 200). This, to me, means that silence should be treated as a discrete and clear-cut category: "Silence is silence and completely different from any kind of language" (p. 200). Besides, silence allows one to attain true meanings (i.e., grasp the essence) of concepts, such as *security* and *freedom.*

I definitely dismiss such approaches to the study of silence as untenable. All linguistic categories are construed theoretically and cannot claim to form *natural* classes of their own outside any continua of linguistic items, such as speech—silence. Thus I will claim that silence and speech do not stand in total opposition to each other, but form a continuum of forms ranging from the most prototypical instances of silence to the most prototypical instances of speech. However, the decision as to which linguistic form should be treated as speech or silence will ultimately depend on a *theoretically* motivated decision of the researcher and not on some natural features of the form in question.

2.4 Communicative and Noncommunicative Silence

This study of silence is—in a very general sense—a sociopragmatic one, that is, I am going to discuss silence as a component of various communicative situations and as a tool of communicative expression. Throughout the discussion I will address the significance of the concept of silence from the perspective of different disciplines. As has been said, I will not attempt to formulate any *final* definition of silence. For the present purposes I am simply going to use the term *silence* as a communicative-interactional category. However, I do not consider all possible types of silence to be communicative. For example, from my operational point of view, muteness will not be treated as a type of communicative-interactional silence. I will also assume that the actual interpretation of someone's silence takes place only when the communication process is expected or perceived to be taking place. For instance, if I pass someone I do not know in the street, and neither of us intends to communicate anything to the other, our respective silences will unambiguously mean that we are strangers and we do not intend to communicate with each other. However, whenever initiation of interaction between us occurs, the silence of either of us will be subject to interpretation. I will use Wardhaugh's (1985) example as an illustration:

> B is a man walking his dog at dusk on a dreary wet autumn evening. His dog, which is on a leash, has just stopped at a building site to relieve himself. B stands waiting, his hands in his pockets. A woman, A, walks briskly, head under an umbrella. Her pace never falters.
>
> **A.** Don't you clean up after your dog, Mister?
> **B.** [Silence.] (p. 198)

A's question is rhetorical, which by definition does not require any answer. But because of the very fact that communication has been initiated, whatever B follows A's question with will be subject to interpretation. The following is Wardhaugh's (1985) assessment:

> B is temporarily lost for an answer, which the comment (or question) uttered by A seems to require. He cannot say *no* since that would be stating the obvious and might sound defiant. He cannot lie and say *yes* since such a lie would be too transparent and, anyway, lying does not come easily even in such circumstances. He can say *Mind your own business* but does not, since, being fully aware of her concerns, he recognizes that it is genuinely part of her business what his dog does—they live in the same city—but he prefers that such business stay private and not be made public. Above all, he does not want to argue with a stranger and it is also quite obvious, from her unbroken pace, that the stranger does not want to argue with him. So B says nothing: his silence or refusal to say something is his response. It expresses his ambivalence and possibly at the same time reassures A in her views: she does, after all, express her opinion on this matter and hears no kind of rebuttal. Even though only one person speaks in this exchange, it has been a cooperative endeavour because the one who remains silent does not seek to contradict or deny in any way the criticism of the one who speaks. Indeed, he tacitly acknowledges its validity. (p. 199)

In this chapter, I am going to suggest that silence together with speech should be considered relevant for the study of communication, of which they both are integral parts. For this reason, I will also reexamine some of the views on silence by other researchers, whose work has been partially referred to in Chapter 1.

2.5 Speech and Silence in Religious Worship

Much work on silence lacks an underlying theory. This often leads to conceptual confusion and obscurity of the argument. Despite valuable observations on the use of silence that they frequently contribute, many studies do not go beyond descriptions of singular facts, which they later generalize into extended, more or less explicit, definitions of silence.

One study that seems to have fallen into this trap is the paper by Maltz (1985). The author compares the noisy mode of worship among the Pentecostals with the silent mode of worship among the Quakers. However, this comparison, which is indeed very interesting, is not the main aim of the paper. Maltz's (1985, p. 114) principal aim is to compare and contrast speech and silence, or, in other words, to describe the meaning of speech and silence.

I have chosen Maltz's paper for a more detailed discussion, criticism, and departure point for my own considerations because he attempts the most elaborate and explicit comparison of speech and silence that I have encountered in the relevant literature. He also makes a number of theoretical claims that seem to me to be very important and basic in studying silence. Let me also add that I disagree with most of them on the basis of my nonessentialist, prototype-oriented approach.

The most important of Maltz's views that will be qualified or argued against in the following two sections are as follows:

Speech (noise) and silence as discrete and opposed categories.

The meaning of silence is invariant.

In communication, speech is normal and silence is deviant mode of behavior.

2.5.1 The Nature of Speech and Silence in Religious Worship

Maltz (1985) very often uses the terms *speech* and *noise* interchangeably without stating clearly if, in the context of his study, they should indeed be treated synonymously. In my view, silence can be contrasted with one or the other, but on adoption of a particular research goal and a theoretical framework, both contrasts should not be confused.

Maltz's discussion of speech and silence is included in the section called "Noise and Silence as Religious Symbols: The Limits of Relativity." The author rejects the view that silence and noise have no nonarbitrary or inherent meanings and denies the possibility of what he calls a *cultural relativist approach* in the study of noise (speaking) and silence in religious worship.[5] This view, however, seems to be totally untenable in light of the following discussion.

In his juxtaposition of speaking (noise)[6] and silence, Maltz (1985) starts off with the interesting statement that "noise and silence represent a continuum of noisiness from zero (silence) to infinity (absolute noisiness)" (p. 130). This promising assumption that speech (noise) and silence belong to one continuum unfortunately does not lead Maltz to treat both concepts as fuzzy ones, and he concentrates on the two extremes of the continuum as if speech and noise were discrete categories. This conjecture guides Maltz (1985) to several important, but in my view mistaken, implications. The first is that "noise and silence both contrast with ordinary social behavior" (p. 130). To me there is no reason why noise and silence should not, at times, constitute ordinary social behavior. One can give numerous examples of noise and silence being regarded as appropriate, normal, and ordinary and talk, or certain forms of talk, being regarded as undesirable or inappropriate. It is rather inappropriate, for example, to talk to strangers in the street by asking them personal questions, unless one gives a good reason for doing so (Milroy, 1987, p. 48). It is appropriate to remain silent during an aria at the opera, at a funeral ceremony, or when one wants to signal hostility to another person. Silence rather than talk is more expected of a subordinate who is reprimanded by a superior. Affection, reverence, attention, hesitation, and other states and emotions are ordinarily and naturally communicated through silence. Likewise, applause, getting someone's attention from a distance, joy, and surprise naturally and ordinarily trigger noisy behavior as does being at political rallies, discos, and many other places and situations.

The next, inevitable question that follows from Maltz's (1985) statement is "What constitutes *ordinary* social behavior?" (Notice the danger of the essentialist, definitional infinite regress.) Of course, the concept of *ordinary* or *unusual* social behavior is a highly relative one, and should have been disregarded by Maltz when a relativistic approach to the study of silence was rejected in the first place. It is also necessary to ask—if *speech* and *noise* are to be treated as synonymous terms—how noisy or soft can speech be before it ceases to be ordinary behavior. Probably the simplest, but again highly relativistic, answer to this question would be that it depends on the context.

Later Maltz (1985) goes on to discuss a "second logical property of noise and silence [which] is that they are opposed to one another" (p. 130). He argues against Baer's (1976) view that glossolalia, silence, and noise may be functional equivalents in religious worship, but he does not explain why he does not accept this view. The only argument that Maltz (1985) uses to back up his point is that

> the logical opposition between noise and silence . . . is that each of them can be used to express opposition to the other. Thus silence is an appropriate response to a world perceived as noisy, and noise is an appropriate response to a world perceived as silent. (p. 131)

I do not doubt that for early Quakers the noise of Pentecostal worship would be perceived as opposition to what they themselves advocated (silent worship), and that Pentecostals would perceive Quakers' silence as a kind of practice that is in sharp contrast with their own. However, the underlying religious goal of both groups during their gatherings seems to be the same—the worship of God. Besides, Quakers' advocacy of the extensive use of silence was motivated by more complex, and less ambiguous, reasons than merely opposition to a world that was perceived as noisy (Bauman, 1983). Maltz describes different sociolinguistic modes of behavior during religious worship among the Quakers, the Pentecostals, and the Puritans. Nowhere does he give any compelling evidence, however, of how these differing modes of behavior should reflect different religious aims of these groups.

Notice that other authors have also claimed that, under different circumstances, various kinds of noise and silence are *functionally* the same or equivalent. For example, Saunders (1985, p. 165) views as functional equivalents *exuberant noise* and *grim silence.* Tyler (1978, p. 84) argues that meditative silence and an uncontrollable flow of words can lead to the same emotional or cognitive state. Finally, Bruneau (1973, p. 20) states that political protest is marked by either "serious silence" or "repetitious chanting," each form lending itself to similar interpretation as ambiguous and undifferentiated.[7]

Also of great interest here is Leach's (1976) treatment of the relation between silence and noise (the latter treated in a wider sense, not specifically as speech) in his approach to the study of culture through a system of binary oppositions. Leach's (1976) statement is especially relevant to the present discussion, because it refers to Bauman's research on Quakers' silence in religious worship:

> Bugle calls and bell ringing mark the time of day; fanfares of trumpets mark the entrance of important persons; gunshots and firecrackers are characteristic markers of funeral processions and weddings; the end of time is to be signalled by The Last Trump; thunder is the voice of God. So:
>
> noise/silence = sacred/profane.
>
> General formulae of this sort pose problems about human universals. Are there some surface features of culture which occur everywhere? I suspect that the answer to that question is "No." Even though some structured relationships among cultural elements are very common there are always likely to be special cases where values get reversed. For example Bauman (1974) has pointed out that it is a fundamental tenet of Quaker theology that God communicates directly with each devout individual who is prepared to sit in silence and await divine inspiration. Here then, in the Quaker case:
>
> silence/noise = sacred/profane. (p. 63)

By using the example of Quakers' silence in worship, Leach demonstrates that when oppositions (here noise and silence) are viewed from a cultural-communicative standpoint, they can switch functions. In this way, he endorses the relativistic approach to the study of what he calls *surface features of culture,* of which silence is one kind.

Maltz (1985, p. 118) states that a born-again Pentecostal student, Michael, whose individualistic attitude to different modes of worship he analyses in some detail, was at one point unsure whether a quiet or noisy style of worship would be more suitable for his individual "spiritual self-exploration." Here the author contradicts himself when he argues that noise and silence are by no means functional equivalents in religious worship. Michael was ready to accept either as his personal style of worship, and selected the one that, in his opinion, suited his personality better. But this shows nothing more than that some people may better pursue their spiritual self-exploration in relative noise and others in relative silence.

One of the most controversial of Maltz's (1985) statements concerning the relation between noise and silence is that

> silence is absolute while noisiness is relative. There's only one kind of silence but many kinds and degrees of noise. Thus advocating noisiness as ideal behavior leads to additional problems beyond those implied by advocating silence. Quaker silence raises problems of purpose and appropriate timing, but Pentecostal noisiness raises questions about how much noise and what kind of noise as well. (p. 131)

In a Quakers' meeting for worship the question of the *amount* of silence involved is present as well. The actual amount of speaking and silence in the 17th-century Quaker meetings for worship varied from meeting to meeting and from period to period. At times there was no talk during a meeting at all; at other times, 2 or 3 hours would pass before someone felt ready to speak (Bauman, 1983, p. 127). Historically, there was also more silence during Quakers' meetings at the beginning of the movement between 1652 and 1654, than from 1670 onward, when more speaking took place during the meetings (Bauman, 1983, p. 125).

Apart from the varying degrees of silence and speech involved in different meetings of the early Quakers, their silence was not qualitatively the same all the time either.

> Not only was silence the state from which all appropriate speaking was to stem in worship, but it was also the ultimate purpose, the desired outcome of speaking. . . . Silence, and especially the silent communion of worshippers, is the most desirable spiritual state for the conduct of collective worship. Any speaking that should take place during worship must emerge from the inward silence of the speaker *and* be directed toward bringing the auditors to silence or enhancing the condition of silence in which they already reside. (Bauman, 1983, p. 125)

Naturally, we may only speculate now whether the early Quakers perceived their silence as only one in kind or whether they distinguished different kinds of silence. However, I would imagine that for someone for whom silence is such an important mode of behavior and communication, there will be more than just one kind of silence. There is, in Bauman's words (p. 125): the "initial" silence and silence as an outcome of the worship process; there is "the silent communion of the worshippers" and "the inward silence of the speaker"; and finally, one can "enhance the condition of silence," which explicitly means that the *quality* of silence can be altered.

Likewise, Scollon (1982, p. 339, 1981) argues that silences (*silent beats*) at the boundaries of tone groups, following their closures, are different in quality from those appearing within a tone group. This supports the claim that silence cannot be treated as a category whose form never changes.

In a way, Maltz's (1985) claim that Quakers' silence is absolute reminds one of the reactions the early Quakers received from

> their contemporaries, who could not understand a religious service being accomplished in complete silence and were apt to see silence as an indication that nothing at all was going on, and thus as a waste of time. (Bauman, 1983, p. 123)

Of course, if silence were an absolute, its every instance would probably be perceived in the same way by everyone encountering it. This may, in some respects, apply to silence understood as an acoustic phenomenon.[8] In any case, in behavioral or communicative terms, different silences will be perceived and interpreted differently. The following lengthy quote from Fox illustrates that people's subjective reactions to silence vary a lot. Naturally, we have to take these judgments into account if we want (1) to isolate the functions of silence specific in a particular community and (2) to find out how the members of a community come to identify these, but not other, functions of silence. The following is Bauman's (1983) quotation of Fox's reaction to those who

> were much against Friends' silent meetings, and sometimes . . . would come to our meetings; and when they saw a hundred or two hundred people all silent, waiting upon the Lord, they would break out into a wondering and despising, and some of them would say: "Look how these people sit mumming and dumming. What edification is here where there are no words? Come," would they say, "let us be gone, what! should we stay here to see a people sit of this manner?" And they said they never saw the like in their lives. Then it may be some Friends have been moved to speak to them and say, "Didst thou never see the like in thy life? Look in thy own parish and let the priest and thee see there how your people sit mumming and dumming and sleeping under your priests all their life time; who keep people always under their teaching that they may be always paying." (p. 123)

Although it is very hard to suspect Maltz of treating Quakers' silence as devoid of any meaning, his comment that silence is invariant, always the same in kind, or absolute presupposes that to him—a viewer from outside—each time it occurs it has the same meaning or function. It seems that his reasoning leads to the conclusion that each instance of silence is undifferentiated from the one preceding or following it. Thus each time silence occurs it can only be contrasted with noise, and not with another instance of silence.

But then, one cannot treat silence and noise (of which speech is a form) as two extremes of one continuum, which is Maltz's earlier claim. While I do accept that noise and silence belong to one continuum, I think that it is theoretically implausible to claim simultaneously, as Maltz does, that any part of a continuum can have clearly, rigidly, and nonarbitrarily set boundaries. If silence is part of a continuum, then it is most likely to have a clear focal point, the most prototypical mode of occurrence, but it will also have different levels of intensity and admixture of noise/speech (fuzzy cases). It can be perceived as coming from within a person's emotional experience or from outside of social rules imposed on an individual. It can be the silence of a computer laboratory, where the clicking of keyboards and printers goes mostly unnoticed by those working there, but where even a quiet conversation is perceived as distracting noise. It can be the anticipatory silence of an audience at a symphonic concert that is just about to begin after the conductor's baton is raised, or the silence of reflection and "awakening" of the audience after the concert, when the orchestra has ended the last note. In these, and other examples, the quality and quantity of silence are subject to change, but what is also very important, the qualitative, and to some degree the quantitative, changes of silence depend on the subjective perception of the individual. Thus what may seem as an absolute and undifferentiated span of silence to one person (the observer) may consist of various, however subtle and inexpressible, silences charged with different overtones and meanings for another (the participant).

2.5.2 The Relativistic and Absolutist Approach: Cultural Stereotypes About Silence

Maltz (1985) confuses two approaches to the study of silence: (1) *relativistic*, in which he treats silence as part of a continuum and (2) *absolutist*, in which the nature of silence is invariant and its meaning nonarbitrary. One cannot advocate 1 and 2 at the same time and claim to be consistent.

The last conclusion drawn by Maltz (1985) from his assumption that noise (speech) and silence form a continuum is that

> the relation between noise and silence is not just a relationship between opposites but between a presence and absence of something such that silence but not noise can be represented as an absence. Thus silence is in a sense a derivative concept: whatever noisiness is seen to entail, silence is a lack of it. Speaking is one of the main expressions of noisiness and speaking—the oral transmission of

> utterances from a speaker to a hearer—has as [*sic*] least three important implications, each of which contrasts with silence: communication, social interaction, and social engagement. (p. 131)[9]

In the next chapter, I will argue that although in their most prototypical meanings the concepts *silence* and *speech* can be treated as formal opposites they both cover a multitude of less clear-cut forms that emerge from situations in which they intersect one with another, and thus the opposition between them is not entirely straightforward. Although it is true that one may be more inclined to describe silence as the lack of speech but not vice versa (i.e., speech as the lack of silence), this is not a sufficient argument to treat silence as a derivative concept. In fact, Maltz's negative definition of silence emerging in the quote above is not an uncommon way of defining pairs of concepts perceived as opposites (why not complements?). A typical sociolinguistic example that should serve as a good analogy here is the way masculine and feminine genders have traditionally been defined and contrasted with each other. Many studies have dealt with aspects of gender and language (in regard to languages that have gender systems based on sex, e.g., English and Polish), pointing out that masculine gender (and thus the male) has been treated by grammarians as the norm in *opposition* to the feminine gender. Subsequently, the latter gender (and thus the female) has been treated as a derivation or deviation from the norm (see, e.g., Cameron, 1985b; Jaworski, 1986; Stanley, 1978).

Instead of treating speech and silence as primary and secondary (derivative) concepts, respectively, I would rather see them as complementary. Tyler (1978) argues that *an act of saying* consists of two basic components: the said and the unsaid. The former component includes the actual utterance and those real and imagined ones that precede it and that follow. The unspoken presuppositions and implications belong to the latter. Tyler also argues in his discussion of the act of saying that its two main components, the said and the unsaid, are on a par with each other in the sense that all the elements of these two components are *reflexively determined.* In other words, they influence each other by contributing to each other's meaning and interpretation by speaker and hearer. The unsaid can be related to Grice's (1975) concept of *implicature,* and it is culture specific. In Malagasy, for example, speakers are less likely to adhere to the *maxim of quantity* ("Be informative") than the speakers in the West. The Malagasy speakers are very reluctant to make exact references to past and future events as well as to mention a third party's name. Thus the expectations of speakers as to what is going to be revealed in someone's speech, and the conversational implicatures will differ in the Malagasy and Indo-European communities (Keenan, 1974).

Let us now return to Maltz's categorical statement that silence is unable to carry communication and provide the basis for social interaction and social engagement. This claim is rejected here in view of the relativistic approach to the study of silence, which means that silence is perceived as a fuzzy concept, whose prototypical meaning varies from community to community. It also entails the view that attitudes to silence as well as beliefs about the significance of silence and talk vary across cultures (Giles, Coupland & Wiemann, 1991; see also §2.7).

One of the Quakers' beliefs about communication, which relativized their conception of silence and speech in regard to others, led them to the advocation of the infrequent use of words. They felt that *carnal* language had so far been inadequate for "true" communication (Bauman, 1983). Consequently, for the language they did use, they propagated a pure or plain style, which was characterized, among other things, by the absence of politeness markers, such as honorific pronouns, greetings, and salutations (Bauman, 1981, 1983). Still, by changing language use and resorting to silence, Quakers did not intend to cease communication but to enhance communication, which they thought had been distorted. Otherwise, they believed, it would be impossible for an individual to attain a spiritual unity with God.[10] For the early Quakers, silence definitely was an appropriate and effective mode of communication, and one can find several passages in Bauman (1983) referring to this fact, as for example: "if your own spiritual power was strong enough, communication could be effected without the overt intention of sending any message at all" (p. 28). And also:

> One often sees in the early Quaker journals the phrase, "he spoke to my condition," to describe the hearer's sense of the striking personal relevance of a Friend's message, seen as a confirmation on both sides of the power of communication in Truth. When spiritual communication was

> taking place, the channel was felt to be open in both directions, and the speaker could sense the responsiveness of others to his message (pp. 28-29).

It also seems that, on a more abstract level, Maltz (1985) expresses a typical Western bias in treating speech as a normal and silence as a deviant mode of behavior. Bias of this kind has been discussed and soundly criticized by Scollon (1985), who argues that more negative qualities are associated with slower than faster speech, with silence than with talk, with long than short pausing, and so on. According to Scollon, in mainstream U.S. society, humans are metaphorically conceptualized as machines, and the constant "humming" of the machine is regarded as a sign of its proper functioning. Once silence takes over from the humming, the (human) machine is perceived as if it no longer worked well.[11] In metaphorical terms—the machine breaks down. In social psychological terms—the individual fails to communicate and maintain social interaction and social engagement.

Such simplistic views on silence cannot be fully accepted even in Western cultures, because the degree of tolerance of silence in conversation varies, even among seemingly culturally homogeneous white Americans (Tannen, 1985). Instead of treating silence as a negative phenomenon with respect to speech, it is more plausible to place silence and speech on a communicative continuum of forms (linguistic items) from most to least verbal. Undoubtedly, most communication involves the use of speech, but this is not to say that silence does not communicate or that when silence occurs social interaction between participants in a communicative event is suspended. I think it is true that to find out how people communicate and what the manner in which they communicate implies it is more essential to study speech than silence. But as a whole body of research on nonverbal communication indicates, the absence of speech does not imply the absence of communication, and very frequently the interpretation of speech itself relies very heavily on the nonverbal component of communication (e.g., Birdwhistell, 1970; Hinde, 1972; Knapp, 1972). Although the most prototypical examples of speech and silence can be treated as formal opposites, I am not labeling them as positive and negative, respectively, as such categorization carries rather evaluative connotations of both concepts. As has already been mentioned, silence and speech complement each other in the linguistic universe and they are capable of performing similar functions and expressing similar meanings. Of course, the nature of communication structured through talk is different from the nature of communication structured through silence (Philips, 1976, see §1.6.3). Different senses are involved in decoding the signals present in both types of communication, and this creates inevitable qualitative differences in the interpretation of the intended messages. To use McLuhan's (1964) handy phrase: "The medium is the message."

As far as religious language itself is concerned, it is often vague, it does not always mean what it says, and it deals with reality in hints. This makes religious language different from scientific language, for example, whose primary aim is achieving clarity and adequacy in its system of reference (Crick, 1976). Besides, religious language is highly ritualized and low in the content of new information. This allows religious language, but not scientific language (e.g., when falsifying a hypothesis), to resort to silence, because silence is ambiguous and susceptible to different interpretations, or as Enninger (1987, p. 273) puts it, following the jargon of information theory, silences (*nonphonations*, in his terms) "are speech segments of high uncertainty." Different degrees of the presence of silence are characteristic in other types of discourse too. For example, as will be demonstrated in §4.4.3, political discourse in the mass media is full of ambiguous and evasive statements. This allows silence to be a prominent and powerful tool of expression in political language. Thus the complex functioning of silence in different types of discourse and its many overlaps with speech point out that speech and silence cannot be treated as *functional* opposites: one being the medium for adequate communication, and the other for creating a gap in communication.

There are obviously good reasons for saying that a very significant function of silence is to indicate the *lack* of any communication and social bondage. But this function can be achieved not only through the use of silence but through the use of speech as well. This is what I will call one of the *negative* functions of silence (see §3.2), even though the same applies to speech (see §§4.2 and 4.3). When speech is used (or manipulated) in such a way that it does not genuinely convey (new) information and/or does not aim at creating social bondage, then the effect of speech is also negative. Thus, following Jensen (1973), I prefer to talk about the positive and negative functions of speech and silence, regardless of the fact that speech rather than silence may be more readily associated with fulfilling positive functions in communication.

In light of what has been said so far, viewing silence as a negative concept and speech as a positive one is, to a large degree, culturally biased. Likewise, the attribution of invariant meanings and interactional properties to either speech or silence does not find plausibility in the communicative realities of different speech communities/cultures. Therefore, a relativistic approach to the study of the meaning of silence has been advocated. Paradoxically, this approach is needed to understand how language, in its abstract entirety, forms a unified system of communication.

2.6 Speech and Silence as Complements

Much of §2.5 was devoted to the argument favoring the treatment of speech and silence as fuzzy, complementary categories, and not as discrete and opposite ones. In this section I will present further supportive evidence showing that speech and silence complement each other, that silence is not a mere background to speech, and that it is not a negative category devoid of communicative properties.

2.6.1 Silence: Keeping the Channel of Communication Open

It is my strong conviction that silence can sometimes signal that the channel of communication remains open, or that one has no intention of closing it, while speech would precisely have the effect of overtly terminating the possibility of further communication between the participants. It is usually thought that the opposite is true—that speech (for example, small talk) is used to indicate one's willingness to communicate with another person and that silence is avoided at all costs to prevent breaking the links of communication (e.g., Burton, 1980, pp. 22-23; Laver, 1981). Observing how people communicate, however, it appears that at times when the participants want to avoid temporary or permanent termination of their communicative process they choose not to say anything for a while, thus feeling secure in maintaining their bondage. Two examples that come to mind are the silent periods before leave-takings and in situations of anger.

When two individuals who are especially close to each other are supposed to part in the street, at the train station, airport, or even speaking on the phone, the periods immediately before the closing formulas are often marked by extended spans of silence. This gives them time to search for the right things to say and simultaneously relieves them from actually saying the definitive words of *good-bye*. When there is nothing else to say it is better not to say anything and to maintain contact and bondage through silence than to overtly acknowledge the inevitable termination of the interaction or relationship.

Likewise, I think some people will react with silence to a situation of anger and severe verbal quarrel. By choosing to withdraw from further verbal exchange of arguments, bitter accusations, and insults, one may prefer to wait in silence for the mutual rage to pass, and then to restart the communication process without the need to repair whatever has been (unnecessarily) said during the argument. It is in this sense that Tannen (1990) analyzes silence in two literary works and identifies the preventive function of silence in restraining outbursts of destructive conflict (see §1.6.4). Of course, reacting to a situation of anger and fighting with silence as a *weapon* is also common. Such silent treatment of the opponent may be even more powerful than uttering the harshest of words and drives many people crazy. Yet, in the long run, the adversaries in an argument may benefit from the relative indirectness and *nonimposition* of silence, which can later help them reestablish contact. In sum, it is possible to identify situations in which silence allows keeping the channel of communication open for future encounters between two or more people, while speech may be felt to endanger the continuation of a relationship.

For example, Bonikowska (1988) uses the term *opting-out choice* in the performance of the speech act of complaint. As one of her informants states, remaining silent rather than uttering a complaint to another party has the benefit of not offending them and avoids the risk of terminating their relationship.

Silence and speech complement each other on a number of planes. As was mentioned briefly in §1.6.2, Philips (1985) distinguishes between two types of communication: one structured through talk and one structured through silence. In many situations in which communication is structured through talk, it is sufficient to rely on verbal signals to understand and interpret a conversation. But sometimes during interaction structured through talk, silence or breaks in speech occur and add to the interpretation of the situation. These are temporary shifts to interaction dependent on physical activities or visual stimuli (e.g., eating, passing food, lighting a cigarette, or reading) or marking a turn-taking juncture. Furthermore, Philips suggests that when interaction is structured through silence, for example, in a dance or a football game, dependence on the visual channel is so great that any talk that *accompanies* the interaction (but does not turn away from it) is secondary to the co-occurring visual stimuli and physical activities.

Without questioning the obvious role of speech in human interaction, it is important to note that in communication talk is simply not always necessary, sufficient, or easy to use. Distracting noise or distance between speakers can make verbal communication so difficult or uneconomical that in some situations it is more effective for conversationalists to rely on nonverbal patterns of communication such as certain visual signals or touching behavior. For example, Kendon (1985) has demonstrated that in such situations gestures, which form "a silent, visual means of expression" (p. 232) can be effectively used in conversation in place of speech. Apart from the reasons mentioned earlier (noise and distance), a party may gesture to add something to a conversation without claiming a whole turn or in place of saying something that is socially awkward.

The following is an example of how a Polish dyad may switch from interaction structured through talk to interaction structured through silence and back to talk again. A husband and wife were driving to a place located some 250 kilometers away from their home. When they got very close to the destination of their trip and they saw a sign informing them that the town they were driving to was only 8 kilometers away the wife said: *"To juz mozna dojsc pieszo"* ("One can make it on foot from here"). The husband joked by slowing down the car and pointing to the door on her side as if to suggest that she should leave the car and start walking. The wife said: "*Wiedzialam ze to zaraz skomentujesz*" ("I knew you were going to comment on it right away.").

In this example the wife's turns were structured through talk and the husband's was structured through silence. His contribution was interpreted without hesitation and reacted to as if he had actually spoken something. She even referred to what he did as a *comment,* which is usually associated with verbal statements. In short, what this situation points out is that interaction structured through talk and interaction structured through silence can exist side by side in a conversation and one can replace the other.

Speech and silence are also intertwined on "lower" levels of linguistic analysis. Cruttenden (1986) lists three major types of places in utterances in which pauses occur: (1) at major constituent boundaries, (2) between minor constituent boundaries but before words with high lexical content, (3) after the first word in an intonation group. Types 2 and 3 typically belong to hesitation phenomena. Type 1, however, has a rather profound role in organizing one's speech into a grammatically patterned and comprehensible structure.

At a discourse level the functional overlap of speech and silence has been observed by Tannen (1987). She notices that repetition has had a rather bad reputation (among nonlinguists) as a highly redundant feature of conversational style. However, repetition serves many purposes in conversation. One such important function is gaining time for planning what to say next. The same effect can be achieved by hesitation, employing filled or unfilled pauses (see also Tannen, 1979). In narratives, the use of repetition rather than hesitation results in the speaker's gaining fluency, and this seems to be a preferred strategy in cultures in which greater value is placed on the continuous flow of speech in conversation than on stretches of silence in a communicative interaction. In non-Western cultures (Tannen, 1987, p. 599, in personal communication with Scollon) or in less industrialized and/or preliterate cultures (Philips, 1985) silence, and not repetition, may be regarded as a more desirable feature of conversational or narrative style. It follows from this example that the relation between speech (e.g., in repetition) and silence (e.g., in hesitation) is not that of positive and negative values and that theoretical accounts of both concepts should not be culturally biased.

Speakers also remain silent in place of a negative verbal response to an invitation or an offer (Davidson, 1984). This usually leads the inviter or offerer to a reformulation of the initial utterance (invitation or offer), which Davidson calls a *subsequent version.*

It seems that, after the initial rejections, when the inviters/offerers are inclined to reformulate their invitations or offers, it is easier for them to do so after silent rather than verbal rejections. "Silence is the extreme manifestation of indirectness" (Tannen, 1985, p. 97), therefore, a rejection of an invitation or offer, which is a highly *face-threatening act* (Brown & Levinson, 1978/1987), performed in as indirect a way as possible (silence), should reduce the risk of face loss of the person extending an invitation or offer and the person who responds to it negatively. In a situation like this, the manifestation of a rejection is communicated successfully through either channel. The silent channel also makes it easier for the refuser to offer a repair following a subsequent version of the invitation or offer. Likewise, the illocutionary force of a complaint can be achieved either verbally or nonverbally, for example, by saying "I hate your smoking around the house" or by opening the window, respectively (Bonikowska, 1988).

Silence parallels speech in performing functions other than rejection. In their analysis of conversational strategies in Bergman's film *Scenes from a Marriage,* Lakoff and Tannen (1984) quote examples of the participants' excessive, irrelevant verbiage and pontification, on the one hand, and of resorting to silence, on the other, to avoid confrontation or discussion of unpleasant topics.

Finally, let us look once again at the role of silence in education (see §1.4.2). Silent periods in a foreign-language classroom in Japan help the students attain a sense of social and emotional balance and integration (LaForge, 1983). In general, silence seems to be a facilitative factor in foreign-language learning in improving the students' reading, writing, speaking, and listening skills. A silent period of delayed oral practice may last 3 months or longer (Muchinsky, 1985; see also Saville-Troike, 1988). Students who are verbally active in the classroom are no longer believed to be better achievers in foreign-language learning than silent students (Day quoted in Muchinsky, 1985). Therefore, even when the foreign language classroom is a silent one and the student spends most time listening to the teacher and to the other students, it does not mean that no learning is taking place. Despite the unfavorable conditions for studying English in Polish high schools (overcrowded classes, focus on grammar and pronunciation drills, continual error correction, and emphasis on rote learning) the students gain a relatively high level of proficiency in English. Due to the adopted teaching mode, the student spends most time in the classroom listening to the teacher and to the other students. This unintentionally induced silent period is a key factor in the students' gaining relatively high proficiency in English (Muchinsky, 1985).

2.6.2 Silence and Small Talk

One more area of communication where silence and speech overlap, however indirectly, is in the case of so-called phatic communion (Malinowski, 1923/1972), or small talk (e.g., Laver, 1981). It is commonly observed that people complain about small talk, saying that it does not form genuine communication. For example, Wolfson (1981) cites foreign students in the United States who do not understand why they do not get invited to Americans' homes, even though the Americans appear to be willing to socialize with them by saying "We must get together sometime," "Let's have lunch together sometime," and so on. Naturally, in situations like these the meaning of the largely formulaic utterances is not the same as the meaning of the sentences (utterances) taken at their face value. Their function is mostly to signal that the channel for further communication is open and that the participants engaging in small talk are full of goodwill to proceed with their friendly relationship.

What appears to be achieved through small talk in one culture need not be achieved in the same way in another culture. For example, Basso (1972) mentions that silence among the Western Apache Indians is used when meeting strangers. It is through not speaking to a newly met person that strangers create a feeling of interpersonal relationship and bondage. When meeting strangers most Westerners try to maintain their conversations uninterrupted by engaging in small talk (Laver, 1981). In terms of Sperber and Wilson's (1986) relevance theory, the contextual effects of both types of behavior—silence and small talk—would be the same. However, to many Westerners the Apaches' silence would mean lack of communication and rapport. Moreover, misunderstandings about the communicative value of small talk are common even among people coming from less diverse cultural backgrounds. For example, New Zealanders find the frequent use of compliments in American English to be insincere (Holmes & Brown, 1987). This is probably due to the fact that in American English compliments have become highly formulaic forms of speech (Manes & Wolfson, 1981), and they perform different functions than in other parts of the English-speaking world.[12]

It appears then that in different cultures and among different members within one culture, variations exist in the degree of necessity felt to engage in various forms of small talk. For some people (cultures), to maintain the impression of the existence of good rapport among individuals, a greater amount of small talk is required than for others. To those who find too much small talk superficial and devoid of true communicative value, remaining in silence in each other's company will probably not be marked as a lack of social contact and integration. Indeed, Giles and co-workers (1991) have reported that Hong Kong students are more positively disposed toward small talk than their Beijing counterparts, and that the latter expressed a greater tolerance for silence than the former.

Milroy (1980) describes how members of the working class in Belfast use silence on informal social occasions. Other rather well known examples often quoted in the literature deal with such uses of silence among Northern Europeans. For example, Lehtonen and Sajavaara (1985) mention that during meals in Finland "silence rather than talk is the rule; it is not considered necessary to be engaged in social small talk while eating" (p. 200). Another example of a rather extensive use of silence in social interactions deals with a different people of Scandinavia:

> The extreme silence of my own experience was with some Lapps in Northern Sweden. . . . We spent some days in a borrowed sod house in the village of Rensjoen. . . . Our neighbors would drop in on us every morning just to check that things were all right. We would offer coffee. After several minutes of silence the offer would be accepted. We would tentatively ask a question. More silence, then a "yes" or a "no." Then a long wait. After five or ten minutes we would ask another. Same pause, same "yes" or "no." Another ten minutes,

> etc. Each visit lasted approximately an hour—all of us sitting formally. During that time there would be six or seven exchanges. Then our guests would leave to repeat the performance the next day. (Reisman, 1974, pp. 112-113)

Even among stereotypically noisy Italians, silence is used in situations marked for deep emotional involvement between family members (Saunders, 1985). In an alpine village, children, for example, learn to retreat to silence in cases when, due to strong emotions, others react less predictably than usual and the situation becomes ambiguous. Silence is also used in this community (as in numerous others) as a preferred strategy for avoiding serious verbal disputes on matters where little or no agreement could be reached.

There is a considerably large degree of tolerance for silence in several non-Western cultures, such as the previously mentioned Western Apache Indians (Basso, 1972, 1979), the Athabaskans (Scollon, 1985), the Igbo of Nigeria (Nwoye, 1985), and the Gbeya of the Central African Republic (Samarin, 1965), and the Amish (Enninger, 1985). All these sources emphasize the fact that in societies that display very extensive uses of communicative silences, the valuation of silence is more positive than in societies in which talk is expected to occur most of the time during an interaction. Among the Warm Springs Indians the lack of an immediate answer to a question does not pose a threat to the flow of communication (Philips, 1976). The answer can be provided later, and often is. The same is true about responding to invitations. The structure of the act of inviting among the Warm Spring Indians seems to be less elaborate and involves less small talk than among Anglo-Americans (cf. Wolfson, Reisner, & Huber, 1983).

> Anglos on the reservation sometimes complain that they are never invited to Indian homes. Some Indians tell them they are welcome anytime, and mean it, but this is not treated as sufficient by the Anglos. Some Indians will tell Anglos that if they are visiting an Indian home, they should not wait to be invited to eat when a meal is served. They should assume there is a place for them and may join the others as they move to the table, if they choose to. (Philips, 1976, p. 91)

It turns out that the concepts of *not enough* small talk and *too much* small talk are culture specific and relative. What may in one culture be perceived as unnecessary or insincere talk may be counterparted as an insufficient amount of talk in another.

Routine or formulaic language constitutes a special case of small talk. Laver (1981) states that "routine behavior is *polite* behavior" (p. 290). He also mentions that one of the three main functions of (routine) phatic communion at the beginning of an interaction is to avoid the awkwardness of silence (see also Bach & Harnish, 1979; Schneider, 1987). It seems then that it has been taken for granted up until now that linguistic routine is verbal. Thus relatively much attention has been devoted to the use of verbal linguistic routines and to certain aspects of routine use of gestures. However, to the best of my knowledge, no one has yet dealt with *silent* routine. The main goal of this section is to argue that some formulaic linguistic (communicative) behavior consists in remaining silent. Silent routine will be discussed with reference to the Brown and Levinson (1987) theory of politeness and Leach's (1964, 1976) cultural anthropological view of communication.

Linguistic routines are commonly used in potentially face-threatening acts (Laver, 1981). The face-threatening acts discussed by Laver in relation to formulaic language include what he calls the marginal phases of conversations—openings, closings, and introductions as well as church ceremonies (baptisms, weddings, and funerals). Because, routine behavior is generally perceived as polite behavior, the use of formulas and ritual language in these situations has the potential of minimizing face threat. Similarly, Tannen and Öztek (1981) observe that one of the three categories of Greek and Turkish formulas involves "anxiety-provoking events" that "seem to occasion formulas for the purpose of creating a sense of control over forces that otherwise seem uncontrollable and threatening. These fall into two categories: *health* and *loss*" (pp. 39-40). Some of the examples of anxiety-provoking events quoted by Tannen and Öztek are choking on food, illness, going on a trip, leave taking, and dying.

Elaborating on Leach's (1964, 1976) anthropological theory of communication,[13] I would like to suggest that each of these situations and events are special in two ways. First, they mark the boundary between two states or activities of a person, for example, not knowing someone and knowing someone (introduction), talking to someone and not talking to someone (leave taking), being here and being there (going on a trip), being a nonperson (in a Christian sense) and being a child of God (baptism), being single and being married (wedding), and so on. Second, they give the participants an ambiguous status: A person choking on food is and is not eating and has hardly any control over his or her body.[14] People getting married are not single any more but not quite married yet, and somebody who is critically ill is not dead but not fully alive either, and generally a sick person is not treated as his or her usual self.[15] As Leach (1976) argues, points of transition and an ambiguous status have a special place in every cultural system:

> A boundary separates two zones of social space-time which are *normal, time-bound, clear-cut, central, secular,* but the spatial and temporal markers which actually serve as boundaries are themselves *abnormal, timeless, ambiguous, at the edge, sacred.* . . . Whenever we make category distinctions within a unified field, either spatial or temporal, it is the boundaries that matter; we concentrate our attention on the differences not the similarities, and this makes us feel that the markers of such boundaries are of special value, "sacred," "taboo." . . .
>
> The crossing of frontiers and thresholds is always hedged about with ritual, so also is the transition from one social status to another. (p. 35)

Thus the use of linguistic formulas typically overrides the use of nonformulaic but otherwise conventionally appropriate language in the most face-threatening situations, and/or in situations perceived as sacred, ambiguous, or taboo. In different cultures and subcultures, different concepts and their exemplifications will be tabooed to a greater or lesser extent. Leach (1964) states that most bodily fluids (e.g., urine, menstrual blood, saliva, etc.) are generally taboo when they leave the body: They are part of someone's body but at the same time they are outside it and autonomous. The degree and force of imposition of taboo on these objects will, of course, vary from (sub)culture to (sub)culture. Take spitting, for example. Skillful spitting (in public) is for some Polish male adolescents an expression of a cool and laid-back attitude, and they will probably see nothing taboo about big (the bigger the better) splatters of saliva on the pavement. This is the case in other cultures as well. In Clemson, South Carolina, an annual spitting contest is organized by the Redneck Performing Arts Association.

Biting nails, or chewing and swallowing them is for some individuals the same kind of habit as chewing gum for others. To most people, however, eating one's own nails is a taboo—nails are not food. Similarly, a lot of people find it improper to make bubbles with bubble gum. What goes into one's mouth should stay there and be either swallowed or disposed of in privacy.

In the same way as various physical objects and physiological functions that, for different people, may connote different values, significance, or a degree of sacredness and taboo, various social situations and events may also be perceived differently by people from diverse cultural or ideological backgrounds.[16]

Some students, for example, consider their graduation ceremony to be an unnecessary formality. They probably do not think of their degree as substantially changing their social or economic status; for them this is not a transition that is worth celebrating. Yet they often do attend their graduation ceremony to give their parents the opportunity to celebrate what they (the parents) see as an important transition in their children's lives. In other words, perceptions of what is sacred, ambiguous, and taboo vary. There is also variation among languages in the repertoires of linguistic formulas available to their speakers as possible reactions to such transitions and ambiguities. In Turkish and Greek, for example, there are more formulas than in English, in terms of both their absolute number and the range of situations which are marked for their obligatory or optional use (Tannen & Öztek, 1981). These differences become especially clear in the speech of second/foreign language (L2) learners, who often apply their first/native language (L1) norms in the use of formulas in the target language or do not recognize the formulaic character of the L2's fixed phrases. For example, a Canadian has reported how utterly perplexed she was trying to close her conversation on the phone with a Pole (in Canada in English), by saying "I've got to go now," and hearing "Where are you going?" in reply (Jaworski, 1990). Fillmore (1984) mentions two cases of misunderstandings of another American English formula: "I thought you'd never ask," which is friendly and teasing, but was interpreted by nonnative speakers of English as insulting expressions of impatience (to an offer of a drink and to an invitation to dance together). Finally, another of Fillmore's examples involves one of his Japanese acquaintances who, on meeting someone for the first time, did not utter the appropriate American formula "I am pleased to meet you" but offered a direct translation of a standard Japanese expression: "This is the first time I have seen you." Comments Fillmore (1984): "While the remark is unexpectedly flattering to people who assume themselves to be well known, it strikes others as being very mysterious" (p. 128).

Languages probably also differ in what I will call *formulaic silence.* Formulaic silence is understood here to be a customary act of saying nothing in reaction to specific stimuli. It occurs when saying something, formulaic or not, would pose a greater threat to another person's face than remaining silent. Therefore, not all instances of silence occurring in place of possible verbal formulas are formulaic to the same degree. When someone sneezes, it is almost a categorical rule in Polish to say: *"Na zdrowie"* ("To [your] health"). In English, "Bless you" or "Gesundheit" is sometimes said in such a situation, but "some people say nothing, and few people mind if they sneeze and nothing is said" (Tannen & Öztek, 1981, p. 38). Here silence is an accepted, conventional, but not formulaic response to someone's physiological bodily reaction. In Turkish and Greek, reactions to events that provoke anxiety result in the use of formulas whose task is to create "a sense of control over forces that otherwise seem uncontrollable and threatening," (Tannen & Öztek, 1981, p. 40). But as I will show presently, not all situations of that kind (specifically, when more or less controllable bodily functions/reactions occur publicly) trigger the use of a *verbal* formula. Why this happens can be explained in terms of Brown and Levinson's (1978/1987) politeness theory.[17]

For example, one will say nothing to a person, even a friend or a relative, who passes gas, has a dripping nose, or coughs out some phlegm and swallows it. The only available formula in situations like these is to remain silent. If one wants to be rude, or ridicule someone, one can say something, but it will not be formulaic.

Obviously, under certain circumstances one can react verbally to someone's passing gas (e.g., when my four-year-old child does it, I ask her to try and control herself), dripping nose (e.g., my close friend whom I want to save from the embarrassment of others noticing it), or coughing (e.g., when I suggest a family member take a medicine to relieve a sore throat). However, one will say it only in the belief that the addressee will not perceive this as a face threat, but as one type of positive politeness strategy: showing concern for the hearer, attending to the hearer's needs and wants. Furthermore, to alleviate the face threat inflicted on the hearer by himself or herself due to "a breakdown of body control, or any *faux pas*," the speaker may joke about what happened or tease the hearer ("God you're farty tonight!") (Brown & Levinson, 1978/1987, p. 104). Another positive politeness strategy in a situation like this can be claiming common ground with the hearer ("We ate too many beans tonight, didn't we!").[18] In the same context the counterpart strategy in negative politeness is to ignore the source of the face threat to the hearer (e.g., his or her runny nose) and remain silent.

It is my contention that a number of instances of ignoring someone's faux pas (verbal or nonverbal) are highly predictable, and therefore, it can be claimed that the silences following self-inflicted face threatening acts are to some degree formulaic. Another connection between silence and speech becomes apparent here. Just as saying nothing that is relevant to the contents of the faux pas (i.e., remaining silent) may minimize the face threat caused by this faux pas, flouting the Gricean (Grice, 1975) maxim of relevance and saying something totally irrelevant to the context may have the same negative politeness effect. Consider the following example quoted by Grice (1975):

> At a genteel tea party, A says *Mrs. X is an old bag*. There is a moment of appalled silence, and then B says *The weather has been quite delightful this summer, hasn't it?* B has blatantly refused to make what he says relevant to A's preceding remark. He thereby implicates that A's remark should not be discussed and, perhaps more specifically, that A has committed a social gaffe. (p. 54)

The use, distribution, and interpretation of formulaic silences, just like verbal routines, is regulated by a set of sociolinguistic rules that involve external, situational factors. For example, in Polish, when a high-ranking superior asks an inferior "*Co slychac?* ("What's new?"), that does not mean that this formula can be returned by the inferior to the superior. Similarly, the patterns of rank and relative status between participants will determine who should remain formulaically silent and when. For example, in a Polish family, when a child belches accidentally after a meal, to alleviate the possible embarrassment of the child and the disgust of others, one of the parents can quasi-formulaically say *"Brzuszek podziekowal za obiadek"* ("The tummy has thanked for dinner") or *"No to dziecko najadlo sie"* ("Well, the child has eaten well."). But when this happens to his or her spouse or some other adult, nobody is expected to say anything. Even when the offender says *"Przepraszam"* ("Excuse me"), a possible response to this apology in other situations—*"Nic nie szkodzi"* ("Never mind")—would be rather rude here. (Unless it can be safely assumed to be an accommodating positive politeness strategy intended to minimize the face threat of the hearer, see above).

Formulaic refraining from speaking appears to differ in kind, depending on whether a given situation is amusing, embarrassing, insulting, and so on, and it occurs in a wide range of situations that can otherwise provide slots for verbal, formulaic, or nonformulaic speech. Let us consider two more examples.

When a group of people sit at a table in a bar and one of them takes leave of the party to play a video game, the others may say "Good luck" or "Have a good game." But when a person takes leave of the party to go to a restroom, the others do not say "Good luck" or anything like that.

In another context, imagine a person having a smudge on his or her face. Even when one does not know this person very well, one can say (nonformulaically): "You have a smudge on your face." The intention of the speaker is for the addressee to notice the smudge and remove it. And such a comment is usually followed by a slightly embarrassed but grateful "Thanks." But if a person has a pimple coming to a head, one would not say anything about it, least of all: "You have a pimple coming to a head on your face."

Formulaic silences do not occur only in situations that do not offer any verbal formulas to minimize face loss. During funerals, for example, the relatives of the deceased typically hear many formulas expressing sympathy, shared grief, or consolation. But it is not uncommon to see in obituaries in the Polish press families' requests like: *"Prosi sie o nie skladanie kondolencji"* ("No condolences, please"). In other words, a request for formulaic silence is made.

Finally, a word on cross-cultural differences in formulaic silence is in order. An excellent example of how the use of this type of silence varies cross-culturally is provided by Basso (1972), whose classic article on silence among Western Apache Indians has already been referred to. Among the Apaches, when strangers meet it is customary for them to say nothing to each other until they feel they have come to know each other well enough to start talking. Likewise, the Cuna Indians of Panama use deliberate silence as *a* greeting pattern (Sherzer, 1977). In these two cultures the ambiguity of the situation and the status of the participants triggers formulaic silence. The same type of interaction in Western culture requires a great deal of (formulaic) verbal behavior.

Of course, it is not clear whether or not Basso would regard any type of silence that he describes as formulaic, but (regardless of any terminological dispute) it is worth noting that they all involve ambiguity or unpredictability with respect to the status of the participants or of the situation. There is also an element of negative face threat involved. Therefore, Basso's ethnographic account of the Apache's silence fits in the theoretical grid of Leach's (1964, 1976), and Brown and Levinson's (1978/1987) work adopted here.[19]

2.7 Conclusion

This chapter on speech and silence has not answered the question of what speech and silence are. As was stated at the beginning of this chapter, no satisfying answers to questions of this type can be given. Instead, I have provided an extensive argument of how speech and silence should be related to each other to avoid the trap of misleading definitional discussions. Much emphasis has been put on the nondiscrete nature of speech and silence and their significant functional overlap. I have argued that, in functional terms, the relation between speech and silence is not simply that of the presence of something and of its absence, that silence can convey various messages as accurately as speech, and that opinions about the negative communicative qualities of silence are culturally biased.

The main theoretical part of this chapter revolved around the presentation of Maltz's (1985) views about silence and their subsequent critique. The position that I have advocated here is that to study silence cross-culturally it is necessary to adopt a relativistic perspective as opposed to an absolutist one. However, I am not ruling out a universalist approach to the study of silence, which I understand as a contribution toward the construction of a unified theory of language on a more abstract level, while respecting the surface differences that remain the driving forces behind diverse human communicative styles and possibly worldviews.

The following chapter discusses silence in such a universalist perspective. The two most important aims set forth in Chapter 3 are to account for the mechanisms responsible for the perception of silence as a meaningful component of a communicative situation and to find a pragmatic theory that will accommodate silence together with speech. Due to the nature of the theoretical speculations in Chapter 3, the cross-cultural differences in the meaning, functions, and beliefs about speech and silence will be disregarded.

Notes

1. This does not mean, however, that I am going to treat speech and silence as clear-cut opposites.

2. See also Vikner (1989) for a brief, related discussion of the relevance of Popper's philosophy to linguistics.

3. An alternative, nonessentialist, approach to the study of speech acts has been presented by Janicki and Jaworski (1990).

4. Consider, for example, two standard dictionary definitions of silence and speech, which could be adopted here as working definitions of both terms:

> **silence** . . . **1:** forbearance from speech or noise: MUTENESS—often used interjectionally **2:** absence of sound or noise: STILLNESS **3:** absence of mention **a:** OBLIVION, OBSCURITY **b:** SECRECY. (*Webster's Ninth,* p. 1096)
>
> **speech** . . . **1a:** the communication or expression of thoughts in spoken words **b:** exchange of spoken words: CONVERSATION **2a:** something

> that is spoken: UTTERANCE **b:** a public discourse: ADDRESS **3a:** LANGUAGE, DIALECT **b:** an individual manner or style of speaking **4:** the power of expressing or communicating thoughts by speaking. (p. 1133)

5. This part of Maltz's (1985) argument follows Sapir's (1937) distinction between referential and condensation symbols. The former are said to be arbitrary and conventionalized, while the latter are nonarbitrary in meaning. Silence for the 17th-century Quakers and noise for contemporary Pentecostals are, according to Maltz (1985), such nonarbitrary symbols, because their meanings are taken very seriously; a multiplicity of meanings are attributed to them; believers feel strongly about them, contemplate their meanings, and expand upon these meanings. In sum, they fit Sapir's (1937)notion of "condensation symbols": the link between these symbols and what they are understood to signify is anything but arbitrary (p. 129).

I have some difficulty in accepting Maltz's interpretation of Sapir's (1937) work. It looks to me to be too far-fetched to claim that Sapir's notion of condensation symbols includes the idea that they are nonarbitrary (although, see Woodley, 1977, for example, for discussion of iconic and indexical signs). In Sapir's (1937) words, condensation symbolism (as opposed to referential symbolism) "is a highly condensed [hence the name] form of substitute behavior for direct expression, allowing for the ready release of emotional tension in conscious or unconscious form" (p. 439).

To me, this implies only that condensation symbols are the kind of phenomena (stimuli) that, in a properly selected context, have more relevance to the participants than other (referential) symbols. In other words, their occurrence has (in a context) great contextual effects and their processing by an individual requires relatively little effort (Sperber & Wilson, 1986; see also §3.5.2).

The above, of course, should not be taken as an essentialist type of discussion over a terminological problem: "What is a condensation symbol?" Instead, it is an attempt to set operational concepts into a theoretical framework. In fact, Maltz's definition of Quakers' silence as a condensation symbol is a shaky one, because it is used outside of its own, i.e., Sapir's (1937) theory.

6. It is not always clear if Maltz (1985) uses the terms *speaking* and *noise* interchangeably or whether he wants to keep them as two distinct categories. To avoid much conceptual confusion, silence should have been *operationally* defined as contrasting with one or the other.

7. Maltz (1985, p. 130) also quotes this idea from Bruneau (1973), but it appears that our interpretations of it are entirely different.

8. However, even in psycholinguistic studies pauses are not defined as mere absences of acoustic signals. For example, Duez (1982) describes a silent pause as "any interval of the oscillographic trace where the amplitude is indistinguishable from that of background noise" (p. 13).

9. Here again, at one point Maltz (1985) contrasts silence with noise and at another with speech (as a form of noise). Unless otherwise noted, I will restrict myself to the contrast between silence and speech.

10. Quakers' exploitation of silence as a reaction to the perceived failure of language is not an isolated example of its kind. Bauman (1983) quotes Sontag who

notes that "Behind the appeals for silence lies the wish for a perceptual and cultural clean slate" (p. 30).

11. Other Western writers have entertained a similar idea of conceptualizing humans as machines. For example, Barthes (1984/1986) sees the ideal of communication in the "rustling" of language (cf. Scollon's, 1986, "humming"): "Stammering (of the motor or of the subject) is, in short, a fear: I am afraid the motor is going to stop" (p. 76). See Popper and Eccles (1983, pp. 4-5) for a critique of conceptualizing humans as machines. It has to be added, also, that Western preference for talk over silence is subject to negative stereotyping in other non-Western cultures. This has been demonstrated by Basso (1979) in regard to the Western Apache joking about Anglo-Americans. "Excessive talk" was a feature of the Anglo-American behavior that featured very prominently in the Western Apache's jokes about the Anglo-Americans.

12. For a brief discussion of cross-cultural attitudes to formulaic language see Jaworski (1990).

13. I will return to Leach's theory in a slightly different context in Chapter 4.

14. The example of a person choking on food is taken from Tannen and Öztek (1981). The Turkish formula used in such cases is *"helâl"* ("it is lawful, legitimate").

Originally, this formula probably implied that one chokes from eating something that does not belong to her/him, without asking permission. The speaker then breaks the "magic" by giving permission to eat the food. (Tannen & Öztek, 1981, p. 40).

15. In support of the present argument it is worth mentioning that a type of institutionalized silence is imposed on the sick among the Aborigines living in the camps near Darwin (Sansom, 1982). Such people are said to be possessed by sickness (hence their status is ambiguous) and thus deprived of the right to talk. When a sick person does talk, his or her utterances are totally discounted and treated as babbling. The words are rejected as having no relevance and thereby become "noise."

16. A very useful and extensive discussion of taboo can be found in Frazer's (1959) classic work.

17. In using this framework I will call *positive politeness* all the politeness strategies the task of which is to show and maintain solidarity between the speaker and hearer. *Negative politeness* covers the strategies of maintaining politeness by avoiding imposition and keeping distance.

18. Trudgill (personal communication, September 1989) has pointed out to me that saying "Cheers!" among British males has become an institutionalized joking reaction to farting.

19. Following Basso's idea, Bock (1976) sees the uncertainty of relations with others as a possible source of silence in Elizabethan culture.

CHAPTER THREE

The Pragmatics of Silence

3.1 Introduction

In the previous chapter, I argued that silence and speech form a continuum of indiscrete items. One extreme of the continuum is dominated by the most prototypical types of silence—meaningful absence of speech—while the other extreme can be characterized by *straightforward* talk. The latter can also be referred to as going bald on record, without redressive action (Brown & Levinson, 1978/1987) or as following Grice's (1975) maxims of the cooperative principle. I have also shown how silence, together with speech, is used in linguistic communication. The aim of this chapter is to use different pragmatic and cognitive linguistic theories to account for the mechanisms governing the use of silence and to back up my earlier claim that in the study of communication, speech, and silence should be treated as equally valid and complementary categories.

3.2 Positive and Negative Values of Silence

When silence is recognized as a possible means of communication, it is typically considered to be able to express a variety of meanings and to perform a range of functions. A number of researchers have pointed out these properties of silence and have indicated that, on a number of planes, silence has two values:

positive and negative. For example, Jensen (1973) discusses five functions of silence and assigns a positive and a negative value to each of them. The functions he proposes are the following:

A. *A linkage function:* Silence may bond two (or more) people or it may separate them.
B. *An affecting function:* Silence may heal (over time) or wound.
C. *A revelation function:* Silence may make something known to a person (self-exploration) or it may hide information from others.
D. *A judgmental function*: Silence may signal assent and favor or it may signal dissent and disfavor.
E. *An activating function:* Silence may signal deep thoughtfulness (work) or it may signal mental inactivity.

Tannen (1985) discusses the "positive and negative valuation of silence" in regard to a number of communicative and social processes. Following Allen (1978), Tannen (1985) says "that silence serves two functions in the literature she [Allen] surveyed, one negative—a failure of language—and one positive—a chance for personal exploration" (p. 94).[1] Furthermore, Tannen lists different types of situations in which silence may function in such an ambivalent manner: either as an expression of good or bad rapport and either as comfortable or clumsy communication.

A similar ambivalence of silence is observed in the cultural-communicative uses of silence in Japanese (Lebra, 1987). The value of silence in Japan derives from the conceptualization of the self as split into two parts: the *inner* and the *outward*. The inner is associated with truthfulness and is located symbolically in the heart and belly. The outward is associated with the face, mouth, and spoken words and with deception, disguise, falsity, and so on, whereas silence expresses inner truth. Reticent individuals are trusted as honest, sincere, and straightforward. Thus silence is an active state, while speech is an excuse for delaying activity.

On the other hand, silence is associated with concealing the truth. When the speaker wants to "gain social acceptance or to avoid social penalty" (Lebra, 1987, p. 347) he or she may refrain from speaking and avoid revealing the outward truth expressed by the spoken word. Social relations with others are governed by complex norms, which depend on social discretion. In sum, as far as inner truth is concerned, silence is the best way of expressing and maintaining it, whereas when the outward truth of the spoken word may be socially harmful and bring about criticism, hatred, or humiliation, silence is the best means of concealing it.

Two other dimensions in the use of silence in Japanese also stand in a type of functional opposition to one another. The first dimension is embarrassment in intimate relations. Young spouses who are deeply in love, for example, often express their affection for each other by nonverbal means and in silence. On the other hand, silence is used as an expression of social defiance in disagreeing with someone, objecting to what has been said or done, or as a signal of anger and hatred.

The ambiguity of silence may be confusing to an outsider trying to make sense out of the silent behavior of others. It may even be difficult for native speakers to interpret and rationalize their own and others' silence in an appropriate manner. Of course, the ambivalent nature of silent communication may often cause misunderstandings. When the pragmatic force of the utterance, in this case silence, attributed by the hearer is different from that intended by the speaker, "pragmatic failure" takes place (Thomas, 1983). It will be suggested later in this chapter that the principle of relevance (Sperber & Wilson, 1986), based on minimization of the information processing effort and maximization of the contextual effects of the utterance, can be useful in explaining how silence is interpreted and disambiguated. However, one has to admit that this can be a difficult task, as in the following examples offered by Lebra (1987):

> It has been shown that silence is not only polysemic but symbolic of logically opposite meanings or emotions. This certainly generates confusion and mis-understanding for a cultural outsider, but for the native as well. The silent speaker, too, is likely to have mixed feelings or rationales. When a woman says she was silent throughout the period of her husband's extra-marital indulgence, she can mean her feminine modesty, compliance, patience, resentment, unforgiveness, or defiance, and may mean all. A man's refusal to express tender feelings toward his wife may be explained not only as embarrassment, but as an expression of male dignity, or as his true, sincere love, which is beyond his words. In the scene of collective decision-

> making, silence can be taken as polite acquiescence or disagreement. (p. 350)

Further ambivalence regarding the nature of silence is demonstrated in English by two common expressions attributing to silence two extremely different qualities: "Silence is golden" and "Silence is deadly" (cf. The Second Foundation, 1982).[2] Sometimes, silence may be regarded as a sign of someone's power or control over others, or it may be a sign of a person's weakness and submission (see chapter 4). Silence may be a state in which one gains knowledge, or it may be a state of idle ignorance or *unlearning*. In love and friendship silence may function as an expression of bondage, or it may be a sign of a disintegrating relationship.

Many other pairs of more and more refined, opposite functions of silence could be listed. Naturally, this bipolar valuation of silence does not eliminate the existence of fuzzy cases—functions of silence falling between the positive and negative ends of each scale. Because all taxonomies of the functions of silence are necessarily open-ended, it is better to leave the formulation of such lists to contexts in which they would serve a particular purpose. For me, it is more interesting to concentrate on discovering theoretical models that can account for all these functions and meanings of silence.

3.3 Traditional Approaches to Silence

That silence is in and of itself ambiguous has been noted by several authors. Different solutions as to the optimal ways of studying its meanings have been offered. Poyatos (1983), for example, argues that in order to be able to interpret correctly a particular instance of silence one has to analyze the verbal context preceding and following it and to consider such features of silence as duration, intensity, and location. A similar taxonomic approach is characteristic of many other studies of silence, called *semiotic*, which have not gone beyond providing more or less elaborate lists of possible meanings and functions of silence (e.g., Dambska,

1975; Johannesen, 1974; Meerloo, 1975; Rokoszowa, 1983; Scott, 1972; Sontag, 1966; The Second Foundation, 1982).

More interesting insights have become available through the application of the ethnographic model to the study of silence in specific contexts and situations (e.g., Bock, 1976; Enninger, 1987; Gilmore, 1985; Lebra, 1987; Nwoye, 1985; Samarin, 1965; Saunders, 1985; Scollon, 1985). Several of these studies have combined the ethnographic perspective with semiotics (Enninger, 1983, 1985), conversational analysis (Tannen, 1985, 1990), and subjects' reports on "beliefs about talk" (Giles et al., 1991).

The most elaborate discussion of the ethnographic approach to the study of silence is Saville-Troike (1985), whose programmatic paper follows the tradition of the ethnography of speaking (Hymes, 1962). Taking a communicative event as the basic unit of the ethnography of communication, we can describe it in terms of its components, and "each component that can call for a different form of speech can also permit or prescribe silence" (Saville-Troike, 1985, p. 14). The author refers to the following components of a communicative event: the *genre*, the *topic*, the *function*, the *setting* (*time* and *place*), the *participants*, the *act sequence*, the *rules for interaction*, and the *norms of interpretation*.

As was stated in §§1.6.3 and 1.6.4, I greatly appreciate an ethnographic approach to the study of silence. However, it seems that Saville-Troike's model, the most convincing of all those known to me, does not go beyond the *description* of communication using silence. What is also needed is a kind of framework that would *explain* and *account for* silence in communication. Just as ethnography of communication has been successful in describing speech and silence, it is possible to adapt certain pragmatic and linguistic frameworks and theories that have primarily dealt with speech, to explain *the pragmatics of silence*.

3.4 The Place of Silence in Communication

To provide further account for the relation between speech and silence arrived at in chapter 2, I will examine a number of different situations in which silence plays a communicative role. In a very general sense, and by analogy to Hudson's (1980) term *linguistic item,* I would like to discuss a range of *communicative items,* which will fall into the category *silence* on the basis of family resemblance features. Evidently this approach is inspired and will heavily draw on the prototype theory (Rosch, 1973, 1975; Rosch & Mervis, 1975). First, let us look at the meanings of some basic verbs referring to silence.

3.4.1 Silence as Absence of Speech and as Absence of Sound

Verschueren (1985) observes that the English phrase *to be silent* contrasts not only with the absence of speech but with the absence of any noise at all. In Polish, there is the verb *milczec* ("to be silent," "to refrain from speaking"), which on the face of it has a narrower interpretation: It stands primarily in opposition to the verb *mówic* ("to speak," "to talk"). *Milczec* seems to have no counterpart in English. On the other hand, Polish has another term which contrasts with the absence of any sound. This is the noun *cisza* ("silence," "absence of sound"). The related verbal form is *byc cicho* ("to be silent," "quiet"). In the following discussion, the main body of examples will be from Polish and I will only deal with silence in the sense of the verb *milczec* and the abstract noun related to it *milczenie* ("silence," "absence of speech") and with those uses of the expressions *cisza* and *byc cicho* which specifically refer to the absence of speech but not to the absence of other types of noise. I will have a little more to say about the other uses of silence in the sense of *cisza* later.

3.4.2 Meaning and Prototypes

I believe that in terms of a commonsense interpretation of the meaning of words (and concepts) at the most basic level of categorization (Rosch, 1978) the meaning of *milczec* ("to be silent") will most typically be associated with the absence of speaking. However, as will be illustrated by the examples below, the words/concepts *milczec* and *milczenie* will also be applicable in situations in which speech does occur. This is because *milczec* resembles "to be silent" in that it may also refer to "habitual reluctance to speak," and the use of this word in reference to a context "does not mean that no words were uttered at all" (Verschueren, 1985, p. 76).

A prototype-oriented analysis of the verb *milczec*, of its derivatives, and of other semantically related expressions will provide the theoretical foundations for the treatment of silence as a complex and indiscrete category. This analysis, which will be presented in the following section, is not intended to be complete; it does not constitute an end in itself, and not all the uses of the verb *milczec* and its related expressions are meant to be covered here. However, I will discuss a range of theoretically possible cases of being silent that will be broad enough to argue that there is no "natural" or "objective" way of separating all the instances of silence from speech. The theoretical corollaries of this hypothesis are the following:

I. The classification of communicative items into silent and verbal ones (i.e., deciding *what* should count as data in the study of silence) has to be a function of a theoretically motivated decision of the researcher.
II. The operational definition of silence depends on, and should be subordinate to, one's research goal and the underlying theory.

3.4.3 An Analysis of the Polish Verb *Milczec*

Consider the following sentences that use the verbs *milczec* ("to be quiet/silent") and *przemilczec* ("to fail to say/mention something"):

1. *Podczas calego zebrania Jan milczal* ("Jan was silent during the whole meeting").
2. *Podczas zebrania Jan zamilkl* ("During the meeting Jan fell silent").
3. *Podczas zebrania Jan przemilczal sprawe deficytu* ("During the meeting Jan was silent about [passed in silence over] the issue of the deficit").

In all these examples, silence is contrasted in one way or another with speaking, and I think it is accurate to suggest that, in terms of the formal properties of silence, the most prototypical meaning of the concept of *silence* involves a total lack of audible vocal signals. However, as will become clear, silence in the sense of abstaining from speaking is relative and gradable. Sentence 1 may refer to a situation in which Jan did not say a single word or produce any audible vocalizations for the whole time of the meeting. But it may also refer to a situation in which Jan did not say anything relevant as to the merits of the meeting. He may have said, for example, "Pass me the handout, please," "Repeat your last sentence, please," or "Wait for me in the lobby." Sentences 2 and 3 clearly involve some talking on Jan's part. From sentence 2 we know that Jan talked for some time at the meeting, and as far as sentence 3 is concerned, Jan may have been the only speaker at the meeting, and he may have talked for the whole time. What follows is that the interpretation of Jan's silence in two out of these three examples allows, or even requires, the assumption that he did at least some talking. Silence, then, can be graded from the most prototypical, (near) total silence of not uttering words to the least prototypical cases of silence perceived as someone's failure to produce *specific* utterances.

However, the amount of talk is only one dimension along which our perception of someone's (or our own) silence is built. The other dimension, which is of equal importance, is whether talk (about something) is expected. Philips (1983) states that "talk is always intentional," (p. 7) and the same applies to *what* is said and *how* it is said. The most common interpretation of sentence 3 should assume that the person who says it expected Jan to talk about the deficit during the meeting. If Jan's speech was not supposed to touch on matters of the deficit, the degree of perceived silence on this topic in his speech would probably be much smaller, if present at all. If Jan did not fail to mention anything that everyone present there thought he should speak about, then sentence 4 would accurately describe his behavior:

4. *Podczas zebrania Jan niczego nie przemilczal* ("During the meeting Jan did not fail to mention anything").

Of course, Jan *was* silent about very many things at the time he was talking (for example, that he had just bought himself a new pair of shoes or that he thought the meeting was a bore or that he had decided with his wife where to spend their next summer vacation) but nobody expected him to talk about them anyway. Our perception of Jan's silence in the interpretation of sentence 4 is so far removed from what we would usually accept as the most typical instance of silence that we would not even think of his behavior at the meeting in any way as silent.

Likewise, sentence 1 will be an appropriate description of Jan's linguistic behavior during the meeting only if there was some degree of expectation that he would or should speak. If Jan had the perceived status of an observer of the meeting, for example, as a journalist, security guard, or porter, one would not choose sentence 1 to refer to the fact that Jan was speechless, but something like:

5. *Podczas zebrania Jan byl cicho* ("During the meeting Jan was quiet/silent").

As has been noted above, *byc cicho* ("to be quiet," "silent") refers generally to the absence of sound. In a situation when one uses this expression to refer to someone's behavior, it contrasts with *milczec* in that the latter expresses the speaker's feeling that the referent was expected to talk but did not. *Byc cicho,* on the other hand, does not imply such an expectation.

Although most prototypical silence involves the absence of speaking, speech and silence are not mere opposites. Just as there are different types and forms of speech, silence will also be perceived as taking different forms, depending on one's expectations toward a given communicative event.

Now consider the following sentence:

6. *Podczas zebrania Jan mówil caly czas* ("During the meeting Jan talked all the time").

This sentence may describe a situation in which Jan, from what everyone recognized as the beginning of the meeting to its end, was the only speaker and talked continuously. One could assume that the author of sentence 6 refers to a situation in which *no* silence was present, but it is not hard to imagine that Jan most likely did pause from time to time: to have a drink of water, to think about what to say next, or when somebody from the audience asked him to repeat a sentence. There is no contradiction of terms here. At the time Jan paused nobody expected him to talk: We do not think that it is physically possible to have a drink and to speak at the same time, there are stretches of time that do not seem to be too long for someone to think about what to say next and not to be perceived as giving up the floor (although the length of time permitted for such pauses will of course vary from situation to situation), and we normally think it is appropriate to stop talking when we are spoken to. Therefore, Jan's pausing during his speech does not invalidate the appropriateness of sentence 6.

That speech and silence should not be treated as absolutes is well illustrated by considering the examples cited so far with the following:

7. *Podczas zebrania Jan nic nie mówil* ("During the meeting Jan did not talk [at all]").
8. *Podczas zebrania Jan nic nie powiedzial* ("During the meeting Jan did not say anything").
9. *Podczas zebrania Jan powiedzial wszystko* ("During the meeting Jan said everything").

Sentences 7 and 8 can both be treated as synonymous with sentence 1, which will be repeated for convenience here,

1. *Podczas calego zebrania Jan milczal* ("Jan was silent during the whole meeting").

depending on whether Jan was actually heard to say anything (sentence 7) or whether he was heard to say something relevant to the merits of the meeting (sentence 8). Sentence 9 will be synonymous with sentence 4

4. *Podczas zebrania Jan niczego nie przemilczal* ("During the meeting Jan did not fail to mention anything").

only if *wszystko* ("everything") is understood in a limited sense of "everything he was supposed to say." To illustrate this point further I would like to compare sentence 9 with sentence 10, below:

10. *Podczas zebrania Jan powiedzial az za duzo. Powinien przemilczec sprawe deficytu.* ("During the meeting Jan said too much. He should have been silent about the deficit.")

Theoretically, what is expressed in sentence 10 is the conviction that Jan was less silent than had been expected. In other words, we can say that speech represents here the lack of expected silence (about something).

As has been noted before, the mere presence of words does not warrant perceiving someone as nonsilent. By the same token, speaking does not always imply saying anything or everything. The Polish verb *przemilczec* ("to be silent about something") is transitive, and it implies that one is silent about something specific, often while speaking about something else, for example:

11. *Kiedy Jan i Maria rozmawiali o zakupach, Jan przemilczal kupno butów.* ("When Jan and Maria talked about the shopping, Jan was silent about [failed to mention] the purchase of the shoes").

There are at least three possible ways of relating Jan's being silent about the purchase of the shoes to the whole situation:

A. Maria knew that Jan had bought the shoes and expected him to mention this.
B. Maria did not know that Jan had bought the shoes, and Jan did not want her to know about it.
C. Jan had not bought the shoes and had not even considered buying new shoes, but Maria thought he had or should have bought the shoes and expected him to mention that.

Notice that choices A and B interpret sentence 11 in such a way that there is the assumption that the speaker intended to remain silent about something. In choice A there is also the hearer's expectation of something to be said, and in choice C there is only the hearer's expectation. Thus not saying anything about the buying of the shoes as described in choice D does not, even remotely, fit the prototype of *przemilczec* ("to be silent about something"):

D. Neither had Jan bought or considered buying new shoes nor did Maria think he had or should have bought any new shoes, so he did not mention it and she did not expect him to do so.

Finally, let us go back to the concept of intentionality of talk mentioned above. Because speech is intentional, so is silence.[3] However, under normal circumstances, we will perceive speech and attach meaning to it even when communication is not expected to take place. But when communication is not expected to be taking place, we will not be inclined to perceive silence as significant and we will not attach meaning to it. In other words, the mere occurrence of words is capable of creating a communicative situation, while the mere occurrence of silence does not. For example, we do not usually expect people to talk to us when they are asleep. If Jan was sleeping and A and B knew that, neither of them would say to the other:[4]

12. *Jan milczy* ("Jan is silent/not talking").

Other things being equal, *milczenie* ("silence/not talking") has only one meaning we can attach to it when we do not expect any communication to be going on at a given time, namely that no communication is taking place. Saville-Troike (1985) states:

> In public encounters between strangers, such as seatmates on a train or airplane, silence may be used to prevent the initiation of verbal interaction, and to maintain social space. (p. 4)

A colleague who recently went on a 5-hour trip by train in Poland told me of an instance of tension created by such *preventive silence*. There were five passengers in her compartment, and apart from the cursory greetings that they all exchanged at the beginning of the trip, nobody said anything to anyone else throughout the whole journey. When they were all leaving the compartment after having reached their destination point, one of the passengers commented *"Jechalismy jak na pogrzeb"* ("We have traveled as if we were going to a funeral"). The situation of sharing one's compartment with the others was probably such that the ensuing silence created a social distance where, for him, it should not have existed, if only for the limited time of the train's journey.

3.4.4 Some Postulates About the Nature of Silence and the Scope of Its Study

The discussion of the most- and the least-prototypical instances of silence in communication allows me to formulate some generalizations about the nature of silence adopted in this study. I am going to do this by suggesting a list of postulates, or principles, that should guide our understanding of silence, rather than by offering an explicit elaboration of my operational definition of silence.

When communication is assumed to be taking place, but the communicator is perceived not to produce any audible verbal signals and this is not interpreted as a violation of any communicative norms, his or her silence is likely to fall into one of the following categories:

i. Silence is a state in which communication takes place (§3.5.1). A given communicative event is structured (Philips, 1985) through, or framed (cf. Tannen, 1979) in, silence. Communication is transmitted through another, most typically visual channel, for example, by means of kinesic or proxemic behavior (e.g., Kendon, 1985). The extension of this framing silence will be discussed in chapter 5 with reference to Edward Hopper's painting.
ii. The occurring silence is formulaic (§2.6.2), and sometimes also accompanied by other nonverbal behavior, such as bowing, smiling, waving, and so on.
iii. Silence is an activity (§3.5.1). The occurring silence is subject to interpretation in the same manner as other instances of linguistic communication following the principle of *relevance* (§3.5.2). A linguistic item becomes classified as an instance of silence when minimal contrast to a formal act of nonspeaking takes place. Implicatures, undifferentiated repetition (nonformulaic), refraining from speaking, and acts of failing to mention something (*przemilczenie*) fall into this category. Visual extensions of silence viewed as an activity will be discussed in chapter 5 in connection with modern abstract painting.

It is not always possible to separate silence from speech very clearly. The interpretation of the message may equally depend on the understanding of both the said and the unsaid elements of the utterance (*implicature*). However, the three types of communicative silence listed above are the most prototypical ones and seem to provide a good starting point for studying silence in interpersonal communication. These categories cover a wide range of forms and situations in which the concept of silence can be used to explain and account for problems of miscommunication and misunderstanding, indirectness, ritualized behavior, and cross-cultural communication.

Apart from listing the categories of the most prototypical types of silence in communication, I would like to mention five other principles guiding the present research on silence. These principles concern the indiscrete nature of silence and point to the study of its less prototypical instances:

iv. Speech and silence are contrasting linguistic phenomena.
v. However, mere absence of speech does not imply the perception of someone as being silent.
vi. Silence (about something) occurs and is perceived as significant and meaningful when talk (about something) is expected by the hearer and/or intentionally withheld by the speaker.
vii. Silence is interpretable when talk is not expected but communication between two (or more) people is assumed to be taking place.
viii. Silence is not absolute, it is gradable.[5]

In view of principles i to iii and iv to viii, I will disregard the unprototypical (though theoretically plausible) cases of silence (*milczenie*) implied by sentences 4, 6, 9, 10, and 12 as insignificant and falling outside the scope of the present analysis. Rosch (1978) maintains that the formation of categorization proceeds along two dimensions: *cognitive economy* and *perceived world structure*. The reason why the situations reflected in sentences 4, 6, 9, 10, and 12 do not belong to the category of communicating in/with silence has to be accounted for by the former dimension: The cognitive effort necessary to perceive the behavior of the actors in these examples as (explicitly) employing forms of silence is too high to be relevant to the context of interpretation. The use of *byl cicho* ("was quiet/silent") in sentence 5 will fall outside the scope of this study because the most prototypical interpretation of the sentence contrasts silence with noise, not with speech.

This theoretically motivated limitation of the present analysis to the types of silence outlined in principles i to iii and modified by principles iv to viii may be different from what others would find appropriate in their approach to the study of silence. For Scott (1972), for example, the types of silence implied by sentences 4, 6, 9, 10, and 12 would probably constitute a valid object of investigation:

> Every decision to say something is a decision not to say something else, that is, if the utterance is a *choice*. In speaking we remain silent.
> And in remaining silent, we speak. (p. 146)

However, I would find broadening the scope of the study of silence to such a degree to be impractical. It would have to account for all the *potential* aspects of remaining silent about an infinite number of subjects in every utterance.

3.5 Theoretical Foundations for the Study of Silence

In his discussion of the semantics of silence, Verschueren (1985) comes to the conclusion that the lexical items and fixed phrases (which he calls *verbials*) that refer to being silent, not saying (something), not talking (about something), and so on are fuzzy categories. He has also claimed that in the languages he has studied, Dutch and English, silence and speech are, at the most basic, central, or prototypical level, treated as opposites and that silence is expressed at this basic level in terms of the absence of speech. This remains in line with what has been said on the relation of speech and silence so far, although it needs to be emphasized once again that speech and silence are not in simple opposition. Verschueren's approach also supports my claim that silence as well as speech are relative categories and that there is no absolute silence, even though one can commonly say:

13. *Pokoj wypelnialo absolutne milczenie* ("The room was filled with absolute silence")

This is where the usefulness of Verschueren's analysis for my discussion stops. Apart from grounding the understanding of silence in the prototype theory, he does not provide any theoretical explanation of what makes silence capable of carrying out different meanings and expressing different functions, and what are the mechanisms of interactants arriving at these meanings and attributing different functions to silence and/or to what is not said. I will now address these issues.

3.5.1 Theory of Metaphors and Conceptualization of Silence

In sentence 13, the speaker refers to silence as "absolute." However, as has been noted earlier (§3.4.3), silence is not itself an absolute, and what sentence 13 really refers to is a kind of silence that the speaker of sentence 13 *perceives* as the most typical member of the category *silence.*

Note also that the way silence is talked about in sentence 13 expresses the speaker's conceptualization of silence in terms of a metaphor: SILENCE IS A SUBSTANCE. According to Lakoff and Johnson (1980),

> We use ontological metaphors to comprehend events, actions, activities and states. Events and actions are conceptualized metaphorically as objects, activities as substances, states as containers. (p. 30)

If Lakoff and Johnson are right, and I think they are, then conceptualizing silence as a substance (as in sentence 13) is possible because we believe that silence is a type of activity. Others have also claimed that silence is not mere inactivity. For example, Samarin (1965) states that "silence is not just the absence of a significant piece of behavior. It is not just emptiness" (p. 115). However, to the best of my knowledge, nobody has yet offered any theoretical explanation of this fact, which I think can be accounted for best by using the Lakoff and Johnson theory of metaphors. Indeed, like any other activity, someone's silence may effect changes in other people's behavior or attitudes:

14. *Marii milczenie wplynelo na decyzje sadu ("Maria's silence influenced the court's decision").*
15. *Swoim milczeniem Maria wywolala wielkie poruszenie ("With her silence Maria caused great concern").*

Consider some other examples which express the metaphor SILENCE IS A SUBSTANCE/OBJECT:

16. *Jan napotkal na mur milczenia* ("Jan met a wall of silence").
17. *Marii milczenie odbilo sie na calej sprawie ("Maria's silence had an effect [lit.: bounced on] the whole matter").*
18. *Zapadlo dlugie, krepujace milczenie* ("Long and awkward silence fell").
19. *Zalegla ciezka, grobowa cisza ("Heavy, tomblike silence fell").*
20. *Przywitalo ja chlodne/obojetne milczenie nauczyciela ("She was greeted by the teacher's cold/indifferent silence").*

Once we treat silence as a substance, we can attribute to it various physical qualities: Silence can be long, heavy, cold or hard (a wall of silence). Of course, like any other substance, silence can be described in terms pertaining to more abstract qualities: tomblike, awkward, indifferent, and so on.

The main consequence of conceptualizing silence as a substance is that we can perceive and describe it as taking different forms. Thus what is most typically referred to as an intentional absence of speech is not conceptualized simply as an activity, but as an activity taking different *forms*.

As far as different functions of silence are concerned, they can be further accounted for by referring to another ontological metaphor, in the sense of Lakoff and Johnson (1980), namely SILENCE IS A CONTAINER. This metaphor embodies another manner of our perception of silence: as a state. Consider the following examples:

21. *Jedli obiad w milczeniu* ("They ate dinner in silence").

22. *Matka wyrazila zgode w milczeniu* ("Mother gave her approval in silence").
23. *Lekarka badala go w milczeniu* ("The doctor examined him in silence").
24. *Przeszli do nastepnego punktu zebrania w milczeniu* ("They moved to the next point on the agenda in silence").
25. *Poddal sie woli dyrektorki w milczeniu* ("He submitted to the will of the director in silence").
26. *Kochali sie w milczeniu* ("They made love in silence").
27. *Wykonywali cwiczenia w milczeniu* ("They exercised in silence").

In all of these sentences, silence is conceptualized spatially and is treated as part of the physical setting of a given activity. We could substitute the expression *w milczeniu* ("in silence") in each sentence with a direct expression of location, for example, *w pokoju* ("in the room"):

21a. *Jedli obiad w pokoju* ("They ate dinner in the room").
22a. *Matka wyrazila zgode w pokoju* ("Mother gave her approval in the room").
23a. *Lekarka badala go w pokoju* ("The doctor examined him in the room").
24a. *Przeszli do nastepnego punktu zebrania w pokoju* ("They moved on to the next point on the agenda in the room").
25a. *Poddal sie woli dyrektor w pokoju* ("He submitted to the will of the director in the room").
26a. *Kochali sie w pokoju* ("They made love in the room").
27a. *Wykonywali cwiczenia w pokoju* ("They exercised in the room").

In all of these examples, *pokój* ("room") is the physical setting of every activity expressed by the predicates, but each sentence will probably evoke a different image of a room most suitable for performing these activities: sentence 21a, dining room; sentence 22a, living room; sentence 23a, doctor's office; sentence 24a, conference room; sentence 25a, business office; sentence 26a, bedroom; and sentence 27a, exercise room.

Because the way we talk about the physical setting of activities (and communicative processes) gives ground for the way in which we talk about silence as a state, it can easily be assumed that we also conceptualize silence as some kind of physical setting. And just as rooms that take different forms can perform different functions, so can different *functions* be performed by different forms of silence.

3.5.2 Relevance Theory

3.5.2.1 Informative Intention and Communicative Intention

In the next step of our analysis of the communicative value of silence, we will concentrate on how the communicator can express different meanings in (state) and with (activity) silence and how it is possible for others to interpret these meanings. To account for the way silence works in communication within a broader pragmatic framework I will turn to the relevance theory proposed by Sperber and Wilson (1986).

In Sperber and Wilson's (1986) model, communication involves two distinct modes: a *coding-decoding mode* and an *ostensive-inferential mode*. While the latter mode may be used on its own, coded communication is only used to strengthen the mode of ostensive-inferential communication. Thus all communication is ostensive-inferential. The communicator is said to use a stimulus with which she intends "to make manifest or more manifest to the audience a set of assumptions" (p. 63).

An important feature of communication emphasized by Sperber and Wilson (1986) is its gradation. Thus verbal and nonverbal communication can be treated as part of the same process, however, assumptions can be made manifest or more manifest to varying degrees. In *strong* communication, assumptions are made strongly manifest, and in *weak* communication, assumptions are made manifest only marginally. According to Sperber and Wilson, nonverbal communication is generally weaker than verbal communication.

The manifestness of assumptions in communication takes place at two levels of intentionality. *Informative intention* is recognized when a certain stimulus (verbal or nonverbal) is produced by the communicator to manifest or make more manifest to the audience a set of assumptions. *Communicative intention* is recognized when it is made mutually manifest to audience and communicator that the communicator has this informative intention. The two basic layers of information provided by ostension are the following: (1) "the information which has been, so to speak, pointed out" (Sperber & Wilson, 1986, p. 50)—i.e., the *informative intention*—and (2) "the information that the first layer of information has been intentionally pointed out" (Sperber & Wilson, 1986, p. 50)—the *communicative intention.* The first layer of information (informative intention) can be recovered without the second (communicative intention).

Let us now look at how the use of silence can be accounted for within Sperber and Wilson's approach to communication as presented so far.

Silence definitely belongs to the nonverbal component of communicative behavior, so in principle it relies on the ostensive-inferential mode of communication and it is weaker than verbal communication in that it cannot make assumptions manifest to an audience in an equally strong manner.[6] This, I assume, is the sole important reason that explains the widely held view that silence is, in and of itself, a highly ambiguous form of communication. Because it does not manifest any particular assumptions in a strong way, it is more open for the audience to speculate about which assumption(s) the communicator had in mind to make manifest or more manifest in his or her use of silence. This also explains why communication has to be assumed to be taking place for a given stretch of silence to be perceived as meaningful. If the communication process is not believed to be taking place, no instance of silence will be able to make any assumption manifest enough to draw anyone's attention.

It should be noted, however, that there are certain uses of silence (e.g., formulaic silence, see §2.6.2) in which the meaning of silence has been conventionalized to the degree that it is more straightforward and less ambiguous than in other, nonformulaic cases. Formulaic silence carries easily accessible propositional meaning (cf. Saville-Troike's quote on pp. 89-90), realized through what Brown and Levinson (1978/1987) have called *conventionalized indirectness*.

Communication with silence makes it possible to fulfill either both the informative intention and the communicative intention, only the former, or neither. With the use of several hypothetical examples (in which I am following Sperber and Wilson's, 1986, use of data), I will now discuss how different forms of silence fit these three types of communicative situations.

First, consider the following:

28. **Peter:** How much do you earn at this new place?
Mary: [Silence]
Peter: Well, you don't have to tell me.

In sentences 28, provided that Mary has heard the question and that Peter assumes that she has, Mary's silence fulfills both informative intention and communicative intention. Peter asks Mary a personal question that she chooses not to answer (verbally). All Peter is left with is Mary's assumption made manifest to him that he should not know how much money she earns (informative intention), and this informative intention is made manifest to him by Mary's ostensively being silent (communicative intention). The assumption made manifest to him in this way can lead Peter to drawing certain inferences that will also be partly dependent on his own, previous assumptions. For example, he can infer that she makes a lot of money at her new place of work or that she makes more than he does or that she makes very little or that she thinks of him as not trustworthy enough to share with him her financial matters. Consider one more similar example:

29. **Peter:** How do you like my new sweater?
Mary: [1-second silence] I love it!
Peter: Oh, you don't like it.

Peter infers that Mary does not like his new sweater despite her saying the opposite because, in the first place, after he asked her the question, she remained significantly silent (dispreferred second), and in the context chosen by Peter for processing her reply, the informative intention of the silence overrode the informative intention of what she said next. Mary's ostensive silence made her informative intention mutually manifest to both of them (communicative intention was thus fulfilled) no matter if she had the intention of criticizing Peter's sweater or not; she may have searched for something appropriate to say for 1 second, which probably made her silence unplanned but nevertheless intentional (see note 3 on this apparent paradox).

It appears that when silence is used ostensively to manifest explicitly (or make more manifest) a set of assumptions, both informative and communicative intentions are fulfilled. In other cases, when silence accompanies other forms of communicative behavior, informative intention can be fulfilled without the communicative intention of the communicator's silence necessarily being realized. A good illustration of this point is provided by one of Sperber and Wilson's (1986) own examples; the hair drier example:

> Suppose . . . that Mary wants Peter to mend her broken hair-drier, but does not want to ask him openly. What she does is begin to take her hair-drier to pieces and leave the pieces lying around as if she were in the process of mending it. She does not expect Peter to be taken in by this staging; in fact, if he really believed that she was in the process of mending her hair-drier herself, he would probably not interfere. She does expect him to be clever enough to work out that this is a staging intended to inform him of the fact that she needs some help with her hair-drier. However, she does not expect him to be clever enough to work out that she expected him to reason along just these lines. Since she is not really asking, if Peter fails to help, it will not really count as a refusal either. (p. 30)

In this example, Mary hides her communicative intention from Peter, hoping that her informative intention will be recognized by him anyway. Mary's ostensive behavior includes remaining silent, although her silence is not intended to make her communicative intention manifest to Peter.

The strategy of fulfilling the informative intention without fulfilling the communicative intention can be easily observed in the case of many instances of *przemilczenie* ("not saying something"). Let's reconsider an earlier example:

3. *Podczas zebrania Jan przemilczal sprawe deficytu* ("During the meeting Jan was silent about the issue of the deficit").

In a situation in which Jan does not want to present his firm in a bad light at the meeting, he may choose not to speak about the deficit. When he talks to an audience unaware of the deficit, his informative intention (i.e., presenting the firm in a positive light) is fulfilled without the audience's recognition of his communicative intention (as has been said before, communicative intention is fulfilled when the informative intention is made manifest mutually to the communicator and the audience). The communicative intention would be realized, however, if some members of the audience were aware of the deficit or if Jan actually said that he was not going to discuss the deficit of the firm (as it might put the firm in a bad light).

As will become apparent in chapter 4 in which *the politics of silence* will be discussed, communicators may very often use silence (also in the sense of deliberately not saying something) in such a way that the informative intention of their ostensive behavior is realized without the audience being fully aware of their communicative intention. Sperber and Wilson (1986) argue that failing to recognize the communicative intention behind the ostension is not absolutely necessary to grasp the informative intention, although not noticing the communicative intention may lead to the failure of noticing relevant information. Because not noticing relevant information by the audience is often the desired goal of those who deliberately stay silent about something, it is clear how silence can be a very powerful source of manipulation of others in face-to-face interaction and in communication on a macro level, for example, in political propaganda and advertising.

Finally, a third type of situation involves cases in which neither informative nor communicative intention is fulfilled, but information is transmitted anyway. This kind of communication is cognitive, not inferential. Consider, for example, gaining information about the speaker's regional origin based on his or her accent. As far as communicative silence is concerned, we can point out the psycholinguistic pauses that have been correlated with certain personality characteristics of communicators. In their overview of studies of psycholinguistic silences, Crown and Feldstein (1985) indicate that the temporal structure of conversation, including the structuring of silent pauses, correlates with self-attributed personality characteristics of speakers: Extroverts tend to have a faster tempo of speech and fewer pauses than introverts. Likewise, the perceived characteristics of the interlocutor (personality traits, race, and gender) lead speakers to the accommodation of their temporal structure of speech, much as conversational silences lead to interpersonal evaluation of communicative partners, although this is also affected by the race and gender of the perceived person.[7]

One of the functions often performed by silent pauses is that of marking hesitation (although hesitation can also be signaled in other ways, such as the lengthening of a syllable, the use of a filled pause, or repetition), and the amount and the duration of hesitation (unfilled) pauses can also be a factor differentiating between various speech styles. In spontaneous speech (e.g., interviews), a greater number of hesitation pauses have been found than in formal speech (e.g., political speeches), although in the latter style unfilled pauses are often deliberately used as stylistic devices, for example, to emphasize the importance of what is going to be said next (Duez, 1982, 1985). It is when conversational silences are ostensively used as stylistic devices that they can be said to have informative intention and, possibly, communicative intention. On the other hand, I will exclude from further discussion psycholinguistic silences (pauses) that are markers of certain underlying personality characteristics and indicators of the temporal structure of speech as being nonexamples of ostensive stimuli.

It has to be emphasized, however, that the separation of this type of silence from the others, which I think are clearer examples of ostensive-inferential communication, is also a theoretically motivated decision (cf. §3.4.2). These silences do stand out as a separate type that can be better accounted for in psycholinguistic terms rather than pragmatic ones, although they share certain characteristics with other types of silence, too. Saville-Troike (1985) calls them *nonpropositional* silences and describes them as follows:

> Another basic distinction must be made between silences which carry meaning, but not propositional content, and silent communicative acts which are entirely dependent on adjacent vocalizations for interpretation, and which carry their own illocutionary force.
>
> The former include the pauses and hesitations that occur within and between turns of talking—the prosodic dimension of silence. Such non-propositional silences may be volitional or nonvolitional, and may convey a wide variety of meanings. The meanings carried

> by pauses and hesitations are generally affective in nature, and connotative rather than denotative. Their meanings are nonetheless symbolic and conventional. (p. 6)

3.5.2.2 Principle of Relevance

In the remaining part of this chapter I will look at how Sperber and Wilson's (1986) principle of relevance is used to explain the mechanisms of communication and will further use their theory in an explanatory model of the study of silence.

According to Sperber and Wilson (1986, p. 54), ostension and inferencing refer to the same process viewed from two different perspectives: The former belongs to the communicator who is involved in ostension and the latter, to the audience that is involved in inference. Inferential comprehension of the communicator's ostensive behavior relies on deductive processing of any new information presented in the context of old information. This derivation of new information is spontaneous, automatic, and unconscious and gives rise to certain contextual effects in the cognitive environment of the audience. The occurrence of contextual effects, such as contextual implications, contradictions, and strengthening, is a necessary condition for relevance. The relation between contextual effects and relevance is that, other things being equal, "the greater contextual effects, the greater the relevance" (Sperber & Wilson, 1986, p. 119). In other words, an assumption that lacks contextual effects in a context is irrelevant, because processing this assumption does not change the old context. There may be different reasons why an assumption would have no contextual effects: (1) the assumption may present new information but it cannot be connected with any old information in the context, (2) the assumption being already present in the old context cannot be affected by the new information, and (3) the assumption contradicts the context but is not strong enough to overturn it.

The second factor in assessing the degree of relevance of an assumption in a context is the processing effort necessary for the achievement of contextual effects. It is a negative factor, which means that, other things being equal, "the greater the processing effort, the lower the relevance" (Sperber & Wilson, 1986, p. 124).

Sperber and Wilson (1986) state that in communication people first assume the relevance of an assumption and then select a context in which relevance will be maximized (it is not the case that context is determined first and then the relevance of a stimulus assessed). Sperber and Wilson observe also that of all the assumptions that a phenomenon can make manifest to an individual only some will actually catch his or her attention. Others will be filtered out at a subattentive level. These phenomena, which have some bearing on the central thought processes, draw the attention of an individual and make assumptions and inferences appear at a conceptual level. Thus they finally define relevance of a phenomenon as follows:

> A phenomenon is relevant to an individual to the extent that the contextual effects achieved when it is optimally processed are large. . . .
>
> A phenomenon is relevant to an individual to the extent that the effort required to process it optimally is small. (Sperber & Wilson, 1986, p. 153)

As has been argued, one of the conditions under which silence is attributed meaning is that communication need be perceived or expected to be taking place. This can now be explained with the help of the principle and mechanism of relevance.

When speech occurs, and regardless of the assumptions that may be made manifest in it that are not "filtered out at a subattentive level," the listener begins automatically to search for a context in which a given utterance will be seen as maximally relevant. Because meaningful communicative silence is, to a great extent, indistinguishable in its acoustic form from noncommunicative silence (e.g., muteness), the identification and interpretation of these two types of silence will have to rely on the functional and psychological aspects of the perception of interaction. Silence is not attributed meaning when it occurs at times when communication is not assumed to be taking place because no one then searches for a context in which it would have any contextual effects. On the other hand, when communication is expected or perceived to be taking place, silence becomes potentially relevant, provided that the audience (addressee) wants to pay attention to the assumptions made manifest in or with silence and that the audience can process this instance of silence with relative ease so that it is going to yield sufficiently large contextual effects for it.

Morgan and Green (1987) pose a more general question: "How could remaining silent be the *most relevant* ostensive stimulus" (p. 727) in a situation in which silence is used? They find this question irresolvable within the Sperber and Wilson approach and hold it against their theory. However, in their reply, Sperber and Wilson (1987, p. 747) suggest that the stimulus being most relevant is not the most crucial aspect of the theory. In fact, the stimulus need only be consistent with the principle of relevance, and in order for that to happen, the interpretation of the stimulus does not have to be maximally relevant for the audience; it must only seem maximally relevant to the communicator (cf. Sperber & Wilson, 1986, p. 169).

Thus the use of silence can be fully accounted for by the theory of relevance. A very good example of instances of silence that are highly relevant to their recipients is provided by Davidson (1984), who discusses the structure of invitations, offers, requests, and proposals when the initial response to them happens to be a potential or actual rejection (I mentioned this example in §2.6.1.). Davidson states that whatever response follows an invitation, offer, and so on, it is perceived by the doer of this act as either an acceptance or a rejection. Silences that occur immediately after the speech act of invitation, offer, request, or proposal are typically interpreted as rejections. When this happens, a subsequent version of the initial invitation or offer is produced in an attempt to cope with this potential or actual rejection. Consider the following example, quoted by Davidson (1984):[8]

[30.] **1 A** Well? I'll tell you. Call information.
2 [silence 1.4 sec.]
3 A We can call information and find out. (p. 103)

In example 30, A expects the other person to communicate either an acceptance or a rejection of the initial proposal. Therefore, whatever follows line 1 has an immediate contextual effect for A, and in this example, the silence is interpreted as a rejection of the proposal. Likewise, the processing effort involved in interpreting the other person's silent response is relatively small, because it immediately relates to the context of the utterance in line 1.

A similar instance of high relevance of silence occurs in formulaic silence, for example, when one does something that potentially may threaten his or her or the addressee's face (as in a faux pas). Whatever response follows afterward will be perceived as either a face-saving or a face-threatening response. In either case, communication is expected to take place, and when formulaic silence occurs it indicates only an apparent lack of communication. What the doer of such a silence really wants to achieve is to make redress to the offender's face. For example, when my stomach starts making funny noises before a formal dinner is served, someone sitting next to me may threaten my positive face by saying something like:

31. Hungry, eh?

But he or she may also ignore the embarrassing noises coming from within my digestive system, in which case I will need minimal effort to process his or her silence about this as making redress to my negative face, and the contextual effects of this person's silence in terms of his or her polite behavior toward me will also be large and fairly apparent to me.

Of course, not all instances of silence will always display such a large degree of relevance in interaction. This will especially apply to situations in which the manifestness of silence is rather apparent to the recipient, but there are numerous contexts from which he or she has to select the one in which an instance of silence would have the greatest effect(s), and thus the effort involved in processing this instance of silence will also be relatively large. Finally, regardless of the amount of effort invested in processing it, a silence may turn out to have very weak contextual effects. Such silences will be perceived as more ambiguous than those with a higher degree of relevance and will be subject to more varied interpretation.

3.5.3 The Relevance of Silence: An Example

McGuire (1985) discusses examples of such largely ambiguous silences, which he calls *open silences,* in his analysis of selected Shakespeare plays and their actual performances.

> An open silence is one whose precise meaning and effects, because they cannot be determined by analysis of the words of the playtext, must be established by nonverbal, extratextual features of the play that emerge only in performance. (McGuire, 1985, p. xv)

In the case of open silences, the play text indicates when a given character remains silent on stage (i.e., when he or she enters the stage but is given nothing to say), and the interpretation of his or her silence is left open to the director of an actual production of the play.

Within the framework adopted here, what happens is that as long as the director of a performance pays attention to whatever assumptions are made manifest in an open silence found in the play, he or she will then start searching (and creating) a context in which this silence will be most relevant. Of course, which context is selected to maximize the relevance of a silence will greatly depend on the overall plan of the staged play that the director has in mind when proceeding to work on it. In terms of Sperber and Wilson's (1986) theory, the set of assumptions and preconceived ideas about the play and its relation to the extratheatrical reality held by the director will correspond to what constitutes the director's context of old information. In general, because all directors' contexts of old information tend to vary, the interpretation of every play (including its open silences) will be different from production to production. Likewise, not all the assumptions made manifest in a play text may be attended to with equal interest by all directors, to the point that some may (and often do) delete parts of the original text in their productions.

One of the open silences discussed by McGuire (1985) is that of Hippolyta's in the opening moments of *A Midsummer Night's Dream.* In one production, her silence was interpreted as a consent to her marriage with Theseus and expressed harmony between the two characters. In another performance, Hippolyta's silence marked her resistance to the male authority of Theseus and her opposition to the marriage imposed on her. In a third production, "Hippolyta's silence was part of a process whereby . . . [she] suspended her initial receptiveness to marriage with Theseus" (p. 9), while a fourth production used the character's silence "to deepen a split between her and Theseus that was present but muted during the play's opening dialogue" (p. 9). Finally, in a television production of the play, Hippolyta did not actually appear on the screen during the scene(s) in which, according to the play text, she should be present although with nothing to say. Thus whatever assumptions Hippolyta's silence may have had for the director of this last performance, he filtered them out, rendering the character's silence irrelevant in the context.

3.6 Conclusion

The above discussion illustrates and explains why silence, in and of itself, tends to be a rather ambiguous form of communication. It also seems reasonable to conclude that if the same principle (of relevance) can be used to explain the mechanisms of human communication with words and with silence, silence indeed belongs to the communicative continuum of linguistic forms from most to least verbal. In other words, it can be identified as the least verbal aspect of linguistic communication and one that is distinct from such nonverbal aspects of communicative behavior as gestures, facial expressions, proxemic and touching patterns, and so on, which will all take special meanings depending on whether interaction is structured through talk or silence, although, of course, they will also add to the interpretation of the communicative process.

Finally, it should also be added that silence per se is neither communicative nor noncommunicative (cf. chapter 2) but that, when examined from the perspective of a given pragmatic framework, it can be communicatively relevant or irrelevant. This is a feature that is also obviously typical of speech.

In this chapter I have shown how the study of silence can be put in a context of more general theories of cognitive linguistics and pragmatics. The prototype theory developed by Rosch (1973, 1978) only has provided a model for identifying various communicative types of silence ranging from the most to the least prototypical cases. The Lakoff and Johnson (1980) theory of metaphors has provided explanation for the fact that instances of silence can be differentiated one from another and attributed different meanings and functions. Finally, the relevance theory of Sperber and Wilson (1986) has been selected as an underlying pragmatic theory in studying the processes of silence interpretation in communication.

In the next chapter, I will use the theoretical premises established in this and the previous chapter to discuss certain applied aspects of the use of silence in certain sociopolitical contexts.

Notes

1. Other authors outside the area of literary criticism have expressed similar views (e.g., Ganguly 1968-1969). However, I believe that the two functions mentioned by Allen (1978) and quoted by Tannen (1985) are not of the same kind. I think that the extreme negative counterpart of the personal exploration function of silence is remaining mute or in a coma, when no conscious thought processes are evidenced. In literary terms, this could be expressed less dramatically as the silence of a writer who has come to have nothing to say. Furthermore, mere use of speech or writing cannot presuppose successful communication, and silence itself may be a successful carrier of a message.

On the other hand, the fulfillment of ultimate bondage and rapport in silence should be recognized as the positive counterpart of the failure-of-language function of silence. In relation to literature, one could give examples of certain uses of silence, or a specific absence of words, to create a desired aesthetic or communicative effect. For example, Petersen (1960) quotes a translation of a Japanese poem accompanying a painting of a flowering morning glory. The flowers of this plant live only for a day. The poem is as follows:

> The morning dawns,
> The night soon follows.
> Life-transient as dew.
> Yet the morning glory, unconcerned,

Goes on blooming, blooming,
Its short complete life.

Petersen adds that the same idea may have been expressed in a *haiku* ending with the words: "Yet the morning glory . . ." This example shows that silence in literature need not necessarily express failure of language (speech), but that it may also successfully carry a message, an image or an idea.

The prominent role of silence in Japanese literature in general has been stressed by Miyoshi (1974). He points out that Japanese culture is primarily oriented toward the visual rather than the verbal element. The subtleties of silence are appreciated more than eloquence. *Haiku* is said to be the perfect embodiment of those ideals in Japanese literature.

2. Such pairing of positive versus negative values on certain concepts or in cognitive systems in general is not only limited to silence. For example, Holowka (1986) has pointed out that in the case of Polish proverbs one can find counterparts of proverbs that when they are paired, side by side, express contradictory messages, for example, *Od przybytku glowa nie boli* ("There's never too much of a good thing") and *Co za duzo to niezdrowo* ("Too much [of anything] is unhealthy").

3. This is not to be confused with the possibility of the communicator producing *unexpected* or *accidental* silences. For example, when my friend tells me that her mother has died, I may remain speechless for some time because I cannot find the right words to say anything, even though I wish I could say something appropriate right away. Therefore, my silence is not quite planned but still—intentional; I prefer to say nothing rather than something that I would find inappropriate to the situation.

4. Howard Giles (personal communication, June 1991) suggests that sentence 12 could indeed be said about Jan during his sleep if he was a nonstop talker and difficult to boot: "At last, he is *not* talking!"

5. I am not going to enter here the theoretical disputes as to whether members of a family resemblance group should be treated as having different degrees of resemblance with their prototype or whether they should be treated as the best exemplars of their categories (closest to the prototype) and less as exemplary items. The second approach rules out the gradation of members of a category as to their common feature (for discussion see Pulman, 1983, and Carston, 1984).

6. Morgan and Green (1987) claim the following: "It also follows from Sperber and Wilson's account that silence cannot be an ostensive stimulus for ostensive-inferential communication" (p. 727). They argue against excluding silence from possible ostensive stimuli. It is not at all clear why Morgan and Green (1987) make this claim because Sperber and Wilson themselves explicitly include nonverbal behavior in their theory and even use "silent" examples.

7. It needs to be stressed once again that the correlation of personality characteristics with pausing phenomena and other temporal aspects of conversational style is often culturally bound.

8. This example appears originally in a transcribed form; here the conventional spelling is used.

CHAPTER FOUR

The Politics of Silence and the Silence of Politics

4.1 Introduction

As was argued in Chapter 2, one cannot oppose speech to silence as a means for carrying out communication versus a state in which there is no communication taking place. Both speech and silence can be used in creating bondage, communication, rapport, and so on, or just the opposite: Both can be used to cut oneself off from others and to convey no (genuine) message. While silence is usually associated with the perception of lack of communication, speech is associated with its presence (Maltz, 1985). In this chapter I want to put more emphasis on some forms of speech that perform the function of noncommunicating genuine messages, of separation of self from others, and of creating the appearance of communication without actually meaning to communicate. I will also argue that silence, understood as a rather broad category, has been used as a tool of sociopolitical oppression and/or control. By discussing these faculties of speech and silence, I am going to explain their mechanisms in a framework developed partly in the two previous chapters as well as in other sources.

I will continue to operationalize silence as a prototype, which will allow me to consider it as a range of linguistic forms. Taking politicians' public speaking, for example, there is not giving public speeches at all and not speaking about specific matters as well as politicians speaking without an audience. I will also fall back on the theory of relevance outlined in the previous chapter to show how certain forms of mass communication (mainly advertising) link up with the negative valuation of silence (as noncommunication). Finally, I will return to Leach's (1964, 1976) theory of taboo for discussion of the ambiguous status and silence of dominated groups, and especially women.

4.2 Absence of Speech and Irrelevant Words

Interpersonal silence has been described in terms of a continuum marked by following two basic forms at each of its ends: "when speech breaks down," and when "words become irrelevant" (Baker, 1955, p. 157). As much as the first form of silence is rather uncontroversial, the latter deserves a comment.

It might be argued that when speech occurs there is no silence. This is not so in view of my understanding of silence based on the prototypical approach to concepts (cf. §3.4.2). Consequently, my suggestion was to account not only for the most prototypical instances of silence associated with the absence of speech but also for the less prototypical occurrences of silence *dependent* on speech, for example, in the sense of *przemilczenie* ("failing to mention something"). The prototype theory allows then to account for different forms of silence associated not only with the lack of speech but also with its use. In this way, silence can be studied as a communicative category and not merely as an acoustic one, and it is possible to incorporate Baker's idea of irrelevant words constituting a form of silence.

Of course, Baker does not use the term *irrelevant* in the technical sense proposed by Sperber and Wilson (1986). However, I would like to use his idea and further elaborate on it within the Sperber and Wilson framework. A marked difference between Baker's approach and mine is that he has concentrated on silence in face-to-face interaction, while in this chapter, I would like to deal mainly with language use in macro contexts. First, I will do so with reference to the language of advertising.

4.3 Irrelevant Words in Advertising

4.3.1 The Language of Pseudocommunication

Various studies have concentrated on the language of advertising—its formal and functional properties. A number of authors have taken an evaluative and thus, generally, a rather negative view of advertising, focusing on its *deceptive* language. For example, Moran (1979) argues that the language of propaganda, including advertising, creates *pseudocommunication* (or *shallow silence* in Capo's, 1982, terminology), as opposed to *communication.* In pseudocommunication the sender of the message is the sole controller of the contents and the meanings of symbols, and there is no negotiation of meaning between the sender and the addressee. The stated and observed purposes of pseudocommunication are in sharp contrast to each other, the former often being hidden or unclear. Pseudocommunication exploits uncritical and collective (i.e., mass-induced thinking), it relies on the passivity of the addressees, and it confuses the symbols and signs with which it operates. This results in the ambiguity of the messages. It makes appeals to emotions rather than to reason and depends on external authorities and secretive and private knowledge. Its means are subordinated to its goals. The universe it presents tends to be uncomplicated and easily understood, lending itself to a simple description in a slogan or a catchphrase.[1]

4.3.2 Relevance, Irrelevance, and Advertising

The addressees of advertising often realize that its language is not that of genuine communication—*information*. Instead they are persuaded to buy something they do not need. A typical reaction then is to disregard the message, at least on the conscious level. And in order for a stimulus to become relevant, it has to catch the intended addressee's attention in the first place or, put differently, the informative intention of the ostension has to be fulfilled (Sperber & Wilson, 1986; cf. §3.5.2.1). A stimulus stands a good chance of going unnoticed or being disregarded at a subattentive level when it is expected to involve a large processing effort or when it is not expected to bring about satisfactory contextual effects. The latter is the case with much of the perception of advertising. An American author states that the adult audiences of television commercials "recognize the routine, know what to expect, and realize that what's coming does not *need* attention" (Goldsen, 1978, p. 363). Goldsen's claim about television commercials is clearly in line with Sperber and Wilson's argument that a stimulus lacks contextual effects if the information it conveys is in no way related to the context of old information, if the information is already present or if it contradicts the context but cannot upset it (cf. §3.5.2.2). This also accounts for Crystal's (1987) claim that

> A walk through the centre of any city places us in contact with thousands of advertisements, in the form of posters, physical models, and neon signs. But it is unlikely that we "see" (that is, consciously register) more than a tiny fraction. (p. 39)

Probably the sheer amount of advertising in industrialized (or urbanized) parts of the world is responsible for the fact that most ads and commercials are filtered out at a subattentive level by the audiences. What I would like to argue here is that just as one does not attribute meaning to silence when communication is not perceived or expected to be taking place, a similar effect occurs with certain forms of spoken or written language, when addressees assume that these forms lack communicative significance for them. This effect of noncommunication is very similar then to the type of silence that appears devoid of any (relevant) meaning.

This is not to say that advertisements always go unnoticed but that their contextual effects may often be too weak to become relevant to their recipients. The fact that such a wealth of products is advertised simultaneously in the United States, for example, creates a situation in which the same types of goods produced by different manufacturers are advertised in the same spatial or temporal vicinity. Consider, for example, the following two pairs of excerpts from toothpaste ads (ad 1a and 1b) and painkiller ads (ad 2a and 2b):

1a. . . . more dentists recommend Crest for fighting cavities than all other toothpastes combined.

It's a point made rather dramatically when you consider that Crest has prevented 523 million cavities since its introduction in 1955 (*People Weekly*, May 18, 1987).

1b. It's a major breakthrough in cavity prevention. Dental schools proved it. With 3 years of new clinical tests. And over 4,000 people. The results were spectacular: New Extra-Strength Aim meant *far fewer cavities than a standard fluoride toothpaste.*

Now the strongest cavity prevention toothpaste you can buy (*People Weekly*, June 8, 1987).

2a. The largest clinical headache study ever against ibuprofen confirms it. Nothing is more effective for headaches than Extra-Strength TYLENOL. Nothing. . . .

TYLENOL does not irritate your stomach the way aspirin and even ibuprofen can (*People Weekly*, May 4, 1987).

2b. More and more people who haven't got time for the pain are switching to MEDIPREN. It works fast, because MEDIPREN contains ibuprofen, the same medicine found in the prescription brand Motrin. Nothing you can buy without a prescription relieves body aches and pain, even headache pain, more effectively. And MEDIPREN is safer to your stomach than aspirin (*People Weekly*, May 18, 1987).

Both ads 1a and 1b state that the toothpaste each advertises is better than all other toothpastes. Both refer to dental authorities (dentists in 1a and medical schools in 1b), and quote long-term medical tests. Using Crest gives "dramatic" results in prevention of cavities, while Aim yields "spectacular" effects. Practically, both ads carry the same message worded in a slightly different manner. If someone accepts one of the ads as true, the other has to be rejected as irrelevant, or at an even lower level of communication, the ad will simply go unnoticed.

Likewise, the two ads for painkillers (ads 2a and 2b) are mutually contradictory in at least two ways:

1. Ad 2b claims that in order for a painkiller to work effectively it has to contain a certain ingredient ("It works fast, because MEDIPREN contains ibuprofen") while ad 2a states that there is a drug without

this particular ingredient that is the best painkiller ("The largest clinical headache study ever against ibuprofen confirms . . . [that] nothing is more effective . . . than Extra-Strength TYLENOL").

2. Both ads attempt to convince their readers that the products they advertise are less harmful to the stomachs of those who take them, which are mutually incompatible claims ("MEDIPREN is safer to your stomach than aspirin" and "Tylenol does not irritate your stomach the way aspirin and even ibuprofen can").

Now when ad 2a, for example, forms part of one's context of old information, ad 2b has a very strong chance of being filtered out. Contrary to the expectations of the authors of the ad, instead of becoming relevant and changing the context of old information of the audience, ad 2b is most likely to remain mute.

It has been argued that speech and silence can be sometimes treated as functional equivalents (§2.5.2). One of the forms of speech in which function converges with silence is repetition (cf. Bruneau, 1973; Tannen, 1987). Advertising provides further examples to this idea. Initially, an advertisement creates a feeling of curiosity; later repetition brings about the effect of comfortable familiarity with the commodity or service. However, after the advertisement or commercial is repeated too long it leads to boredom and disgust (Bogart, 1984, p. 217).

Advertisers are, of course, aware of the possible silence or muteness in communication effect created by the frequent repetition of ads and commercials. Here *silence* refers to a communicative vacuum created by extremely low relevance of the stimuli. Therefore, new advertising campaigns for the same products and services are launched time and again. Producing new stimuli, advertisers try to create new contextual effects for their audiences. Sometimes a given commercial is aired only once, as was the case with the visually spectacular—and spectacularly expensive—commercial that introduced Macintosh computers to the U.S. market. More commonly, a television commercial is repeated frequently up to the point at which a new commercial for the same product is released, often featuring a new catchphrase, tune, or image by which the product or service is expected to be remembered better.

4.3.3 Repetition in Political Propaganda

Political propaganda often uses strategies adopted from advertising. Sometimes it takes exactly the form of advertising, as exemplified by television commercials for presidential candidates in the United States and preelection commercials of the Conservative and Labour parties in Britain. For propaganda to be successful, it has to function continuously for an extended period of time (Ellul, 1965). However, there is a limit to the amount of repetition necessary, and indeed desirable, for propaganda.

> Hitler was undoubtedly right when he said that the masses take a long time to understand and remember, thus it is necessary to repeat; but the emphasis must be placed on "a long time": the public must be conditioned to accept the claims that are made. In any case, repetition must be discontinued when the public has been conditioned, for at that point repetition will begin to irritate and provoke fresh doubts with respect to former certainties. (Ellul, 1965, p. 17, n. 9)

In other words, when such a communicative vacuum created by indiscriminate repetition of the same propaganda clichés is maintained for too long a time, the audience may find new, undesirable contextual effects following from it. This is similar to the type of prolonged public silence of a politically powerful person, organization, or government when talk is expected but does not occur (cf. Brummett, 1980, and see below).

4.3.4 Artistic Exploitation of Repetition

The intended, repetitive nature of some of Andy Warhol's films leads to another effect of creating a type of communicative silence. I am not using the term *communicative silence* here in the negative sense of noncommunication, but of communication *through* silence. For example, Warhol's 6-hour long *Sleep* (made in 1963, showing one man sleeping) loses—or in fact, it never acquires—a story-telling quality, due to its repetitive nature and relatively motionless imagery. Probably for the first time in the history of filmmaking the audience was not expected actually to watch the film for the entire time of its screening, which is not to mean that the audience was intended to be programmatically disinterested in the film. Although the first public screenings of *Sleep* were sold out, the auditorium was usually only half full. The film audience walked in and out of the auditorium during the showing to have a hamburger, chat with others, or smoke a cigarette. After a time, viewers could go back to watch the film for a few minutes again and contemplate a new image or shot of the sleeper's body. However, apart from the level of silence the film created on this only apparently noncommunicative (i.e., nonliterary) level, the film's silence had yet a different effect on its audience.

> *Sleep* has its own temporal pace, of course, and a very different one from our own. But we slip in and out of that time at will. It is a meditative time, erotic, almost necrophilic, while ours is—well, our time is our own, and perhaps the clock's. The movement—and it is our *own* movement—from one temporal realm to the other is among the major sources of interest, and incident, in this masterpiece of quiescence. It is the meditative pleasures of dissociation that the film proposes to us. Its time and ours are not melded but irresolvably contrasted, and the operation of that contrast from minute to minute gives the film its life. (Koch, 1973, p. 40)

In sum, it can be said that excessive repetition may create an indiscriminate series of noises equal to indiscriminate noncommunicative silence. But repetition, especially in artistic endeavors, may also bring the audience to a higher, meditative-like level of consciousness, reflection, and understanding.

4.4 Silence, Politics, and Society

4.4.1 Political Strategic Silence

In political discourse, silence is also recognized as a tool, not only an effect, of certain strategies employed to achieve particular goals. Brummett (1980) analyzes the theoretical implications of *strategic silence,* illustrating it with the example of 10 days of such silence from President Jimmy Carter (from July 5 to July 15, 1979). Strategic silence in politics is defined as:

> the refusal of a public figure to communicate verbally when that refusal (1) violates expectations, (2) draws public attribution of fairly predictable meanings, and (3) seems intentional and directed at an audience. (p. 289)

The difference between political strategic silence and other forms of communicative silences is that the former does not have to rely on its context to make its meaning predictable, whereas the meanings of the other kinds of communicative silence can only be interpreted in relation to the verbal and other nonverbal context in which they appear. The *political* context of strategic silence always results in the creation of *"mystery, uncertainty, passivity* and *relinquishment"* (Brummett, 1980, p. 290). From one perspective, the aura of the mystery around a powerful political leader may add positively to the public's general image of that person. More often, however, the silence of a person who is expected to deliver speeches, appear on television, and be seen in public places may have the opposite effect: creating the image of a weak, passive, and helpless person. Politicians who are expected to talk to the press a lot but do not are picked apart about that, as in the following, somewhat humorous, commentary:

> **Andy Rooney:** Newspaper and television correspondents at the White House complain that President Reagan hasn't had enough press conferences. Are the reporters right? Well, here are the statistics on presidential press conferences, beginning with Franklin D. Roosevelt. He had a total of 998 press conferences. Of course, he was in office for 12 years, but still that's an average of 83 a year. Truman had 324, an average of 40 a year. But look at these statistics. Nixon only had 37, averaging six a year, and that's what Reagan has had, only six press conferences a year while he's been in office.
>
> President Reagan seems to prefer the helicopter press conferences because he can't hear the questions and the reporters can't hear the answers with the helicopter's engines running, the blades whirring, the dog barking and the tourists singing "God bless America." (CBS News, 1987)

In evaluating the outcome of strategic silence it is necessary to analyze the political contexts preceding and following the silence, its ethical aspects, and other nonverbal behavior accompanying it as well as other factors. Then it is possible to describe and evaluate the role of a strategic silence and decide whether it has achieved its goals and whether it has had a positive or negative influence on a given person or group. In other words, was the mystery, uncertainty, passivity, and relinquishment created by the silence desirable, or should it have been avoided?

In his critical account of President Carter's strategic silence, Brummett (1980) concludes that it turned out to have been an undesirable move for the president: Carter's low ratings from the period before his silence plummeted even more.

4.4.2 Rose Garden Strategy

A different instance of Carter silence,[2] which at least initially won him great support and improved poll ratings, has been discussed by Erickson and Schmidt (1982). This time, Carter's silence lasted for several months (in 1980). However, it was not a total silence as in July 1979. Instead, for several months Carter chose to withdraw from political discourse related to the 1980 election campaign. The direct cause of this withdrawal was the crisis of the U.S. hostages in Iran:

> I want the world to know that I am not going to resume business as usual as a partisan campaigner out on the campaign trail until our hostages are back here, free and at home. (quoted in Erickson & Schmidt, 1982, p. 402).

Erickson and Schmidt's (1982) aim is to discuss nonstrategic (see note 2), political, presidential silence in an election year with respect to "campaigning, confronting opponents, and partisan issue-taking" (p. 404). This type of silence is referred to as *the Rose Garden strategy*.

The conditions facilitating the use of the Rose Garden strategy include the following: (1) the existence of an external crisis (in Carter's case the hostage crisis) that justifies the concentration of a president's attention exclusively on this particular issue, (2) identification of a common external enemy, (3) recognition of the importance of the issue as worthy of attention, and (4) the public's belief in the president as able to resolve the crisis.

The outcome of the Rose Garden strategy for the president may be either positive or negative. The presidential benefits may include the presentation of himself as competent and strong enough to perform his presidential duties; attaining a mythic, positive identification; creation of a special bond with the electorate; showing sacrifice of his own career for the nation's sake; and upsetting his political opponents by refusing to communicate with them. The possible drawbacks in adopting the Rose Garden strategy include the exact opposites of the potential advantages: political isolation and creation of an image of a weak and passive president without a program and unable to take up a dialogue with his opponents. (For a detailed discussion of these issues and their illustration through examples from Nixon's, Ford's and Carter's presidencies see Erickson and Schmidt, 1982.)

Strategic silence and the Rose Garden strategy are interesting to compare with respect to the principle of relevance. Both appear relevant to the public but in different ways. Strategic silence involves great processing efforts by the intended audience: No one really knows why a public figure or institution should suddenly remain silent. However, no matter how vague they may be, the contextual effects produced by such strategic silence are very large: The feeling and aura of mystery, uncertainty, passivity, and relinquishment is created almost instantly and is very profound. Thus strategic silence warrants relevance due to the contextual effects it produces.

The Rose Garden strategy, on the other hand, is highly relevant due to the low processing effort it requires. As was stated, this type of silence is announced and explained beforehand and the public has no difficulty in identifying its source and its stated goals. However, the contextual effects of such silence for the public are rather minimal.

4.4.3 The Significance of *Przemilczenie*

In §3.4.3 *przemilczenie* ("not speaking about something," "failing to mention something") was recognized as a possible form of silence. It was also suggested that this type of silence is particularly well suited for political manipulation of others, on a personal level, as well as on a societal level.

An example of a community in which this is an apparent feature is that of the Barundi (inhabitants of Burundi) (Albert, 1964). Upper-class boys receive special formal training in speaking correctly, elegantly, and appropriately, whereas upper-class girls receive careful training in maintaining "artful silence and evasiveness." They are expected to be able to listen very carefully to what is said about their families and later to repeat it verbatim to the males in the household. The verbal skills in which the females are trained, and in which they excel, are "bargaining and negotiating skills for use behind the scenes" (Albert, 1964, pp. 37-38). Two proverbs common among the Barundi are "The man who tells no lies cannot feed his children" and "Truth is good, but not all that is true is good to say." Thus the Barundi are very self-conscious about different forms of speaking and about what is said. Their well-being depends, to a great extent, on what is (not) said, and how it is not said. Discretion is the key concept in maintaining one's security. Discretion manifests one's loyalty to a superior, often in hope of reward, and it involves a more or less overt use of silence:

> The need for discretion, a halfway house between literal truth and bald lie, is understood as either not speaking at all about delicate matters or as refurbishing facts so that they wear an innocent face. (Albert, 1964, pp. 46-47)

On a theoretical level, Albert's study provides an important illustration of my earlier claim concerning the gradation of silence. Among the Barundi *przemilczenie* ("failing to mention something") clearly involves different *degrees* of not saying something or being silent. Moreover, it turns out that what is *not* said directly is more important and carries a greater informational content than what *is* said directly.

> Cultural skill in inventing and interpreting figurative speech and allusions is general, but indirect reference also operates to define boundaries between in-groups and out-groups in various situations. At a princely court, a man may sing a tale full of allusions understood only

> by the prince himself or only by a few of those present. The incomprehensibility of the allusions is in itself meaningful. Listeners know something is in the wind, and they are not slow to inquire and to find out. If the information were not intended to be made public, it would not have been presented at all; if it were common knowledge, the allusions would not have been incomprehensible. Like the rhetorical technique of strict silence, the poetic technique of not quite telling has positive information content of great significance. (Albert, 1964, p. 50)

Of course, discretion is only one form of verbal indirectness and should not, by any means, be restricted to the Barundi. On the contrary, various forms of indirectness, involving the concept of *przemilczenie*, are employed for different reasons universally (Brown & Levinson, 1978/1987).

Maintaining silence over certain issues often is a major political tool for control and imposing the status quo. It is probably a universal that taboo topics exist for every political power no matter how democratic it tries to appear. For example, despite *perestroika*, which had been going on in the Soviet Union for several years, in 1989 the centrally controlled Soviet press kept silent about several world events of great international importance: condemnation of Iran for sentencing Salman Rushdie to death, Romania's policy toward its Hungarian minority, General Noriega's conflict with the Panamanian opposition, condemnation of the Chinese government for the student massacre in early June 1989, and Bulgaria's policy toward its Turkish minority. (*Gazeta Wyborcza*, 1989, p. 6)

At times, public figures decide to exert some kind of self-censorship. It is often quite easy to identify ("No comment") and it may even be openly admitted that certain information will not be disclosed. Such was the case when the Reverend Jimmy Swaggart scandal was uncovered, which involved Swaggart's dealings with prostitutes. After his testimony before the Assemblies of God, Swaggart was offered a rehabilitation plan. Announcing what the plan included, Cecil Janway of the Assemblies of God finished his statement in the following way:

> Again, no doubt much speculation and rumor will find its way into the secular media, but for the church, the body of Christ, such

> speculation and rumor has no place. We urge Brother Swaggart and his associates to resist the requests of those outside the church to respond to questions. (ABC News, 1988a, p. 3)

The host of the television program "Nightline," from which the above quote is extracted, tried to make sense of the decision of the Assemblies of God to let Swaggart preach again after only a 3-month break (even though the whole rehabilitation period was to cover 2 years) and directed his doubts to one of the program participants. The following exchange took place in which the host, Ted Koppel, showed clearly that the self-imposed self-censorship of the Assemblies of God is a powerful tool in playing political games:

Koppel: . . . I tend to be kind of cynical, and when I hear a two-year rehabilitation but, that he can be preaching again in three months, I say to myself, here's a man who brings in $150 million a year for his church, and while the rehabilitation may go on for two years, the church doesn't want to close down that kind of income. Am I being too cynical?

Richard Dortch, Former PTL president: Yeah, I think you are, Ted, and I'll tell you why. The problem that you and I have is that we don't have the details, all the information that those church officials have, and those are godly men. They're good men. They're reasonable men. And I'm sure that if you and I knew all that they know, we would probably come up with the same decision as they have.

Koppel: Yeah, except there's that wonderful point at the end that Mr. Janway made, and that is, not only that Jimmy Swaggart should refrain from talking to anybody in the media, but basically he was suggesting to all members of the church who are in possession of any of the facts that they should not talk. Now, it's one thing to say, if you only knew the facts, folks, then you might understand the decision. But to say, if you only knew the facts, but whatever happens, we're not going to tell you the facts, that kind of puts you between a rock and a hard place, doesn't it? (ABC News, 1988a, p. 3)

The next example of self-imposed self-censorship comes from another "Nightline" program. In the following, of necessity, lengthy excerpt Girma Amare, an Ethiopian diplomat, gives very evasive—and for the most part irrelevant—answers to the questions he is asked. Because he cannot say nothing and, probably, because he does not want to contradict Ted Koppel's suggestions of the inefficiency and corruption of the Ethiopian government, Amare chooses to evade the real issues, which are the main concern of the program.

When Koppel asks his question about the possible corruption within the Ethiopian government, Amare states how tragic the situation in his country is, which is obvious, and which is why the program is devoted to Ethiopia. Then, instead of speaking about the government Amare talks about the weather and the drought, again saying the obvious. The government is mentioned in the context of a request for international aid. This is probably intended as an attempted refutation of Koppel's claim that the Ethiopian government is so corrupted that it does not care for the people of Ethiopia. When Koppel repeats the question about what the government is actually doing to improve the situation, Amare starts talking about the limited resources of the government and the fact that Ethiopia as a developing country is singled out as the responsible factor. *Repeated* appeal for international aid shifts the emphasis away from the role of the government to the problem of famine but without mention of its sociopolitical context. In a reference to the government, Amare notes that it is doing its best to distribute the food in the areas affected by the drought, but this is too general to be relevant. Likewise, instead of giving Koppel a straight answer to his question about the possibility of a temporary truce in Ethiopia, Amare starts to blame some unnamed "elements" for disturbing the transportation of food, and finally gets carried away in a propaganda speech about the democracy flourishing in his country.

Koppel: . . . Mr. Amare, critics of your government, both internal critics and external critics, point to the inefficiency of the economic system, they point to the fact that your government is spending an exorbitant amount of money on a huge army rather than spending money on development. To what degree is what is now developing again in Ethiopia the fault of an inefficient system and a corrupt government?

Girma Amare, Ethiopian Charge d'Affaires: It is quite a pity that the fate of people who have been threatened by drought is taken for a political end. The fact of the matter is that the summer rains have suddenly stopped to come to the northern part of Ethiopia and some other regions of the country, and the result of that was there was a shortfall in the expected harvest, and for this reason, the Ethiopian government, in order to prevent any kind of catastrophe that has reached during 1984 and 1985 has taken it upon itself to appeal for the international community, at least, to take some preventive measures.

Koppel: And I'm sure, Mr. Amare, that the international community will respond again, as it did three years ago, but three years ago there were also instances that just mystified people in the west. Food that lay rotting in warehouses while people were starving miles away, an exorbitant, extravagant celebration in your capital city at a time when people on the outskirts of the city were starving to death, those kinds of things cannot be separated. I fully understand that you're talking about a tragedy that is developing here for which the people are not responsible, but I'm not asking you about what the people have done. I'm asking you about what the government has done.

Mr. Amare: The Ethiopian government, with its limited resources, has alloted [sic] at least, all its resources to the distribution of food, to the effective distribution of food within the country. But as you know, as a developing country, Ethiopia has very much economic limitations. We don't have enough transportation means, and we don't have the facilities to transport this food from the ports to the hinterland of the country. As a ragged country, there is lack of enough roads within the country, and for this reason we have appealed, besides food, at least for transport for the trucks so that this food will be delivered.

As much as the government is concerned, at least it has given its top priority for the distribution of relief food within the country and the Relief and Rehabilitation Commission, which has won an international reputation for an effective and efficient distribution, at least has strengthened its capacity at present, at least to take food from wherever it is delivered to the closest places which are affected by the drought.

Koppel: I realize, Mr. Amare, that the war, for example, with the Eritrean rebels has been going on now for almost a quarter of a century. Would it be possible at a time like this for a temporary truce, so that food could be distributed?

Mr. Amare: As you know, there are always certain elements who are always bent on to disturb the smooth flow of food within the country, but at least with the proper cooperation with the government and with the Relief and Rehabilitation agency, the food can be, at least it can be taken to those places and you might know that in Ethiopia, at present, the new republic has been declared and there is a new constitution, which guarantees rights and privileges and which grants civil and political rights to the people and which would provide original autonomy to the different nationalities.

Koppel: Forgive me for interrupting, but if you are going to talk about that, I'll start to talk about the 25,000 political prisoners. Let's stay for a moment, at least, on the distribution of food, and let me ask Mr. Seiple [president of World Vision USA], who was just in your country, I didn't really get a straight answer to the question I asked, let me see if you can provide an answer for me. Is it possible that some kind of truce could be arranged between the warring factions so that food could be distributed, or is that out of the question? (ABC News, 1987, pp. 5-6)

In this example, the intent to refrain from speaking about certain matters is not openly admitted. Actually, every effort is made to give the impression that all which is said during the program is relevant and exhaustive. Nevertheless, despite the efforts of the interviewee to bury the sense and relevance of the interviewer's questions in the multitude of words, the evasiveness of style is detected by the interviewer.

Another example, which more specifically deals with the use of euphemisms and also averts the attention of the public from what really is at issue (here, the invasion of another country), is provided by Nixon's "Cambodia speech" (delivered on April 30, 1970), quoted in Boardman (1978):

Confronted with the situation, we have three options.

> First, we can do nothing. The ultimate result of that course of action is clear. Unless we indulge in wishful thinking, the Americans remaining in Vietnam after our next withdrawal would be gravely threatened. . . .
>
> Our second option is to provide massive military assistance to Cambodia. Unfortunately, . . . massive amounts of military assistance could not be rapidly and effectively utilized by the small Cambodian army against the immediate threat. . . .
>
> Our third choice is to go to the *heart of the trouble.* That means *cleaning out* major North Vietnamese and Viet-Cong occupied sanctuaries. (p. 82; emphasis added)

In this excerpt, Nixon employs features of persuasive style, which aims at gaining support for a cause unnamed directly. Instead of suggesting "Support our plan to invade Cambodia," he conditions the listeners to arrive at this idea as their own. He gives them three options of what can be done in given circumstances, of which the last is clearly the one he desires the most. However, he uses euphemisms to refer to attacking the Vietnamese troops in Cambodia ("go to the heart of the trouble"), and killing them ("cleaning out").

4.4.4 Oppressive Silence and the Status Quo

Silence and silencing measures have been used by political dictators and dictatorships to exert control over dominated groups in various parts of the world and at different periods in history. A kind of macro silence is the desired state for most political dictatorships. Kapuscinski (1976) notes that silence is an indicator of misfortune and crime, and allows tyrants to do anything they desire as long as their activities are not exposed to the public, commented on and protested against: "Notice how well silence was maintained by every colonial power; with what discretion the Inquisition worked; how Leonidas Trujillo avoided any publicity" (Kapuscinski, 1976, p. 91).

The same author also makes a point of the role of the mass media in maintaining the politically desired state of silence and through it, maintaining the status quo. Gibberish fed to the viewers, listeners, and readers of the mass media successfully averts their attention from the real issues and problems of their countries.

> If I tune my radio in Guatemala to a local station and I only hear songs, beer commercials and a single item of news from the world saying that Siamese brothers have been born in India, then I know that this radio station works in the service of silence. (Kapuscinski, 1976, p. 91)

Naturally, this quote can be directly related to the identification of irrelevant words as a form of silence discussed above (§§4.2 and 4.3).

In most recent history, an effective way of silencing opposition in various countries has been the introduction of martial law. In the early 1970s the martial law declared by President Marcos silenced the Philippines' opposition and enabled the president to consolidate power (Bruneau, 1973). Similar temporary silencing measures were applied in Poland on December 13, 1981. The imposition of martial law allowed the authorities to induce literal and metaphorical silence in the country by stopping most forms of public communication. The broadcasting of regular television and radio programs was suspended and so was the publication of all newspapers and magazines. The telephone lines were cut, and domestic and foreign mail was officially censored. Universities, theaters, and cinemas were temporarily closed. Several thousand people were imprisoned and public gatherings were banned. Traveling within the country was highly restricted, and travel into and out of the country was virtually impossible. The imposition of silence and relative social stillness were the key instruments that enabled the authorities to introduce this new law and old order in the country.

The silence of oppression is a desirable state for all power groups that are afraid that the mere expression and exchange of opinions or the free flow of information will threaten the existing status quo. This is why there are often legal measures introduced for not allowing political opponents to speak out. For example, before communism in Poland collapsed, underground publications were destroyed because their contents "posed a threat to national security"; small fliers and pamphlets of a political nature, which were distributed in the streets, were confiscated and the people distributing them were charged with littering.

Perhaps one of the most blatant forms of silencing oppressed groups is not so much to deny them access to the media, but to deny the media access to these groups and to the events revolving around them in a given country. An ABC News "Nightline" program discussed these issues, with respect to three countries: South Africa, Israel, and Panama. At the time of the broadcast (March 1, 1988) the governments of these countries had considered or actually denied access of the foreign media to the scenes of uprisings and unrest. The following excerpt illustrates how such silencing works in practice:

> **Rose [ABC News correspondent]:** [The] Israeli government . . . recently has given serious consideration to official banning reporters and cameras from the occupied territories. And late last week, the army began taking steps to do just that.
> **Israeli Soldier:** No pictures now.
> **Rose:** What does your order say?
> **Israeli Soldier:** After that you can, but now, not at all.
> **Rose:** What is your order?
> **Israeli Soldier:** Anything.
> **Rose:** Tell me what your orders are.
> **Israeli Soldier:** Let's go now, okay?
> **Rose:** What, we can't shoot here?
> **Israeli Soldier:** You can't stay here. You can't stay.
> **Rose:** You're telling us we can't go inside.
> **Israeli Soldier:** You must stop at this one.
> **Rose:** Your orders are to keep the news media out?
> **Israeli Soldier:** Yes, yes, I told you. Wait here. (ABC News, 1988c, p. 2)

When the power group cannot pretend to act within the confines of the existing law, it may turn to more or less open acts of terror, such as in the case of the *desaparecidos* ("the missing people") in some Latin American countries (see §4.5.5).

Another effective way of using silence to achieve certain political ends is to maintain information control by way of censorship.

Those who use it try to justify their actions through the use of double-talk. That it is an effective strategy is illustrated by the following example:

> At the height of the guerilla war, a Rhodesian farmer's wife complained, over dinner in a heavily fortified homestead, that the death of Steve Biko had been used by the Western press "to give South Africa a bad name." Silence is the safest guarantee of reputation; the safest guarantee of silence is to wipe out the mind. (Caute, 1986, p. 5)

The silencing of a group may take very subtle but equally effective forms: brainwashing, indoctrination, and negative stereotyping, which all lead to the creation of a group's self-image as a powerless, submissive, inferior body with nothing relevant to say.

4.4.5 Breaking the Silence of Oppression

Silence is oppressive when it is characteristic of a dominated group, and when the group is not allowed to break its silence by its own choice or by means of any media controlled by the power group. An obvious example is political opposition groups in some Eastern European countries, which for many years did not have (and in some cases still do not have) access to government-controlled media; another example is opposition writers whose books are not published by official publishing houses. In both cases, the solution was to publish underground papers and books or to publish with foreign companies, broadcast underground radio programs, or simply and effectively, to make use of the medium of graffiti[3] to communicate brief messages to many people at once. In all of these cases, the breaking of the superimposed silence is beyond the preventive control of the power group.

4.4.6 Women's Silence

Many aspects of the oppressive role of silence in politics can be related to the societal silencing of dominated groups. I would like to devote this section to a discussion of oppressive silence of one such group: women. Apart from identifying the problem, I will also explain the mechanisms of silencing women within a wider framework applicable to the study of other oppressed groups as well (§4.5.3).

Silence has been a prescribed state for women for centuries, as exemplified in the well-known admonition by St. Paul:

> Let the women keep silent in the churches, for they are not allowed to speak. Instead, they must, as the Law says, be in subordination. If they wish to learn something, let them inquire of their own husbands at home; for it is improper for a woman to speak in church. (II Cor. 14.34-35).

In the opinion of many authors, women individually or as a group have been silenced in many ways. Amundsen (1981) argues that in their early struggle, the U.S. feminists of the 1960s were silenced by the simple fact of lacking access to the male-controlled media. Zimmerman and West (1975) and West and Zimmerman (1983) discuss the interpersonal silencing of speakers in cross-sex dyads.[4] Their research shows that females are frequently interrupted in face-to-face conversations by males, but not vice versa. Baron (1986) states that women have been kept in a double bind. On the one hand, they have been expected to talk to fulfill a part in social life, and on the other hand, women have been expected to remain silent to conform to their status as men's inferior.

Kramarae (1981) discusses the linguistic position of women from the point of view of Ardener's (1975) *muted group theory*. Women have lost their language and have become inarticulate; they have been forced to adopt the male (the dominant group) perception of reality together with the masculine language that describes and represents this reality. The silencing of women has taken many forms: "namelessness, denial, secrets, taboo subjects, erasure, false-naming, non-naming, encoding, omission, veiling, fragmentation and lying (Rich quoted in Kramarae, 1981, p. 25; see also Houston & Kramarae, 1991).

Daly (1973, p. 93) refers to two kinds of *great silence:* (1) over women's achievements in a patriarchy-controlled history and (2) over the "arguments for and evidence of the matriarchal period."

By contrast, women whose silence tends to be a sign of reticence and submission have less opportunity to indulge in the relaxing, private silence that men have access to at home (Sorrels, 1983), and the common silence of male inexpressiveness has been viewed as a peculiar sign of men's political domination over women (Sattel, 1983; Sorrels, 1983).

A discussion in the British press of the differences between males and females (Watts, 1988) has also stressed the use of silence by men as a tool of domination in communication. Although it is commonly assumed that women have superior verbal skills to men, it does not mean that women are in control of the communicative process. On the contrary, as Watts (1988) notes, the power game that goes on in communication of feelings is won by inarticulate and silent men with the following statements: "You know I'm no good with words," "I can't explain how I feel," "What do you want me to say?" and "Don't you *know* by now that I love you?" (p. 33).

On a sociopolitical level, the silencing of women as a group has been rather successful. It has worked so well that even the significant voices of many women in the past have been silenced and have become forgotten. Spender (1982) presents evidence of the many women who, for centuries, have been written off in the history of education and science. Probably the best indicator that the process of silencing women has been successful is that many women themselves do not perceive any kind of feminist tradition in their lives and work. As Spender argues, this tradition exists but has been concealed in the workings of a male-dominated education system.

The same idea of the lack of a recognizable tradition of women's activity in the past, and a resulting feeling of alienation and indeterminacy of one's self from others, is present in Rich's writings. Like Spender, Rich (1979/1984, p. 11) also observes that women's efforts to gain self-determination have been continuously silenced.

Consequently, the breaking of silence by women has been viewed as a positive change toward their emancipation. In line with what has been said in the previous section, women have chosen certain radical and unconventional means of breaking their silence so that they could escape the control and censorship of the power group. Amundsen (1981) claims that at the time of the radicalization of the feminist movement in the 1960s the only certain way to get access to the male-controlled media was to be newsworthy (see below).

As to literary style, a tactic of a different kind has been adopted by many writers. The aim of a number of feminist writers has become twofold: to convey radical messages of women in changing times and to alter the language of literary expression. The main points of the argument concerning the change of language (or style) is as follows. Traditional language was made by men, for men. Therefore, women have no language of their own—they are "silent." Even if women try to speak out and express their feelings, experiences, desires, and so on, the masculine language is inadequate for this purpose. The language of the oppressor leaves many concepts and problems simply unnamed, and the experiences of men and women are different to the point that they need different forms of linguistic expression (e.g., Daly, 1978; Kramarae, 1981, 1992; Spender, 1980; see also Olsen, 1978, for a collection of feminist literature on the topic of women's silence).

Penelope and Wolfe (1983) observe that the literary tradition of 20th-century women writers is that of silence. It is "a tradition of closely guarded, personal, revelatory language of diaries and journals" (p. 125). The authors discuss a few modern writers (Maud Haimson, Mary Daly, Virginia Woolf, Gertrude Stein, and others) who have broken the literary silence of women in the 20th century and who have all used alternative modes of discourse, instead of traditional, patriarchal language patterns. One such experimental mode of expression is silence itself, which is featured prominently and especially in Woolf's work (cf. Mendez, 1972, 1978, 1980).

> Silence is important in Woolf's work in three major ways: (1) *Communications*—her characters affirm the significance of silence in human relationships, suggesting at times that the truest part of communication goes on in the silent dialogue, in the silence of love; (2) *Style*—her novels make use of silence stylistically by concentrating on the spaces between events, thoughts, words, and by deliberate use of imagery and lyrical language to evoke in the reader a feeling of silence; (3) *The Mystery of Being*—in exploration of the metaphysical dimensions of silence, Woolf's entire works bow to the eloquence of nature, light, and unheard music, directing the reader to the silent mysteries of life, death, and selfhood. (Mendez, 1980, p. 95).

Thus feminist writers create their own style(s) of expression. Apart from exploring the communicative and symbolic values of silence they break their own silence and speak with new voices. They introduce into their writing elements of intuitive knowledge and associative thinking; they rely heavily on the use of neologisms; and they rename old concepts, alter the meanings of words (often based on their etymology), and alter syntax (Penelope & Wolfe, 1983). Another recent feminist challenge concerns the authority and prescriptivism of the male-controlled dictionaries and the word meanings defined in them (Kramarae, 1992).

4.5 A Theory of Sociopolitical Silencing

So far I have argued that silence is used as a tool of sociopolitical oppression and that women as a dominated group have been silenced in various ways. This is commonly assumed to be a sign of their oppression by men. But such considerations can be put into a wider theoretical perspective. In doing so I will provide a general explanation of the mechanisms governing the silencing process of minorities, and apply it to the silencing of women and other groups. I will refer here to Leach's (1964, 1976, 1977, 1982) cultural anthropological theory of societal organization. Notice that this is a further elaboration on the theory that I mentioned in §2.6.2, where I suggested that formulaic silence is a frequent response to what is perceived as behavioral taboo resulting from the ambiguity of someone's status or action. This idea can now be extended to the more general context of sociopolitical relations.

4.5.1 Taboo and Society

It is taken almost for granted in cultural anthropology that human thought and social structure are organized along the lines of simple, binary oppositions, for example, I/other, we/they, dirt/purity, friend/enemy, and silence/noise. In a world structured in oppositions of this kind, humans attach the status of normality to everything they perceive as simple, intelligible, and logically ordered, in contrast to the abnormality of that which is disorderly and unintelligible. The perception of a feature as normal or abnormal is never a question of objective fact but of the circumstances in which it is observed, for example, "sexual activity, which is in itself a normal part of normal life, can suddenly become abnormal when it is classified as 'dirty' " (Leach, 1982, p. 115). And it follows that

> whatever is felt to be abnormal is a source of anxiety. Abnormalities which are recurrent and frequent become hedged about by cultural barriers and prohibitions which have the force of signals: "Danger; keep out; don't touch!" Breach of such prohibitions constitutes the prototype of moral evil; the essence of sin is disobedience to a taboo. (Leach, 1982, p. 115)

This is why self-identification almost always involves the negative identification of others. As Leach claims, the "true" humans have the same eating habits as us, they follow the same conventions in regard to sex relations, and they dress like we do; others ("nonhumans") do not. I believe that one should add to Leach's list one more important characteristic by which people tend to differentiate *us* from *them:* the former speak an intelligible language or its accepted variety, while the latter use an unintelligible language or a "corrupt" version of the "right" language.

It is quite easy to assume that the perception of another person or a group of persons can be altered or manipulated. If I want to perceive someone as same or as different, it is my decision to do so. A person's status can be made clear to me in two possible ways: I can perceive him or her as a member of my own community or of a clearly different one. In both cases, his or her status will be definite to me and I will accept it as normal. It does not cause me anxiety. However, the identity of a person can be altered so that he or she will be perceived as someone who belongs neither to *us* nor to any accepted and unambiguous *others*. Such an ambiguous status can be attributed to two types of individuals or groups: (1) those who are perceived as unfit for any group approved of by the existing status quo (outcasts or rejects) and (2) those whose identity is redefined for various political reasons (e.g., striking workers being described as "law breakers" or "heroes fighting for democracy").

The main reason why it is possible to redefine one's status and, even more important, make it ambiguous is that social boundaries have fuzzy edges. Consequently, social concepts overlap and these overlapping areas are, by definition, ambiguous. Following the examples quoted by Leach, such entities as *Man* and *God* and *Life* and *Death* involve intermediate concepts, respectively, of a mediator, "a god-man towards whom all religious ritual is addressed and who is thought of as the source of metaphysical power" (Leach, 1977, p. 17), and "sickness where the individual is neither altogether alive nor altogether dead" (1977, pp. 17-18).

Moreover, the individual's ambiguous status can also be manipulated, depending on the situation. Take criminals and policemen, for example. According to Leach, both have an abnormal status because they represent an intermediate state between the society at large and its individual members. Criminals can be said to be the mediators between the society and its members defined as rebels, whereas police officers (heroes or rulers) mediate between the society and the ruled. In the act of breaking into a private house by a criminal and by a police officer, for example, the treatment of an individual as a criminal or a police officer "will depend, not on the facts of the case but what we *believe* to be the case with regard to the legitimacy of the situation" (Leach, 1977, p. 16).

The mechanisms involved in the sociopolitical process just referred to are the same as in the space-time relations universally operating in various cultures. For example, as Leach states, the time slots in which changes of one's status take place, from child to adult, from unmarried to married, from sick to healthy, and so on are nobody's time. They are marked by ambiguity and, therefore, call for ritual. I will repeat the same quote that appeared in §2.6.2:

> A boundary separates two zones of social space-time which are *normal, time-bound, clear cut, central, secular,* but the spatial and temporal markers which actually serve as boundaries are themselves *abnormal, timeless, ambiguous, at the edge, sacred.* (Leach, 1976, p. 35)

Here, I am drawing an analogy between spatiotemporal processes taking place within culture and certain political processes taking place within society. In Leach's anthropological terminology, ambiguous-abnormal groups such as sorcerers, priests, rulers, criminals, and the sick become a taboo. My claim is that in sociolinguistic terms, when such groups are oppressed, one of the manifestations of their taboo status is that they become silenced.

4.5.2 Altering the Status of Dominated Groups and Political Opponents

When the position of a power group is potentially or actually threatened, this group often chooses not to engage in genuine dialogue with the dominated groups (the source of the actual or potential threat to the status quo) to defend its position. Instead, the opposition's voice is suppressed (silenced). To do this, the power group must alter the society's perception of the status of the opposition from clear to ambiguous. One effective way to do so is simply to question the opposition's right to exist, to ban or delegalize it, or to declare it subversive. Frequently, when the existence of a sociopolitical opposition or dominated group is acknowledged, this is accomplished by labeling and describing it in terms that completely alter its status. A similar effect of an ethnic minority becoming "invisible," or being without a clear voice of its own, appears when its self-image is distorted, as has been observed in the case of the Mexican minority in the United States (National Educational Association, 1972).

4.5.3 Women's Ambiguous Status, Subordination and Silencing

As a dominated group, women have frequently and consistently been victims of a policy leading to the establishment and perception of their status as ambiguous. The theoretical framework adopted here predicts that the combination of these two factors leads to the silencing of women both as individuals and as a social group. The present section provides several examples of how women have been oppressed and how their status has been made ambiguous at the same time, all resulting in inflicting silence on women. The next section will illustrate the same process in regard to the Solidarity trade union in Poland in 1980-1981.

Beginning, appropriately, with ancient Greece, we find Aristotle's view that "women were deformed males" (Hill, 1986, p. 42). In the Judeo-Christian tradition women have been caught up in the double status of a sinful Eve and a sinless Mary (Daly, 1973, p. 82; see also an important discussion of the ambiguous status of the woman in Christaian mythology in Leach, 1976, pp. 73-75). The woman is often conceptualized as a prostitute/sex object (Pace Nilsen, 1986; Stanley, 1977), although it is also true that derogatory comments about one's mother's sexuality is among the worst—ritualized or not—insults in Western and other cultures (e.g., Bronner, 1982; Cubberly, 1984-1985).

An excellent analysis of the silence characterizing women in 16th- and 17th-century Britain is provided by Belsey (1985). Although she does not refer to Leach's work, her approach stands in full agreement with it. Belsey maintains that women occupied "an uncertain place" with respect to their status on a number of levels. In the family a married woman's identity depended on her relationship to her husband. Legally, only unmarried women or widows enjoyed economic independence. When married, a woman was treated in relation to property like a child—women were "not legally recognized. . . . Neither quite recognized as adults, nor quite equated with children, women posed a problem of identity which unsettled the law" (Belsey, 1985, p. 153). The status of married women was also unclear regarding their position of authority: being a mistress and a mother meant having authority over servants and children, respectively, as was the case with being a master and father. But being a wife meant for a woman subordination to her husband's power and authority. Such uncertainty as to the woman's place and status resulted in two types of silence: the silence of women as a sign of their submission and the silence of women as a reaction to their ambiguous (taboo) status. Should women be talked about or discussed in any meaningful, relevant terms, they would have to be unambiguously identified as women, and this would pose a threat to the identity and coherence of the male status quo world. Belsey (1985) observes:

> Men are to command, servants and children are to obey, but a woman is to govern and not to govern, present as example or surrogate, but absent from the place where decisions are made.
>
> In the family as in the state women had no single, unified, fixed position from which to speak. Possessed of immortal souls and of eminently visible bodies, parents and mistresses but also wives, they were only inconsistently identified as subjects in the discourses

> about them which circulated predominantly among men. In consequence, during the sixteenth century and much of the seventeenth the speech attributed to women themselves tended to be radically discontinuous, inaudible or scandalous. (p. 160)

Moving on to the present times we can find further examples of how the status of contemporary women has been ambiguated and, coupled with their subordinate position in society, effectively used to silence women individually or as a group. Brownmiller (1975) presents compelling and oftentimes shocking evidence of the politics of rape. This is not the place to summarize the whole book, the main, and excellently corroborated, thesis of which is that rape "is not a crime of lust but of violence and power" (Brownmiller, 1975, back cover). What is of special interest to my argument is that, as Brownmiller argues very convincingly, the victims of rape, who are predominantly women, usually remain silent about the crime that has happened to them. Their silence is not voluntary; it is the silence of the shame and fear that they anticipate in case their rape case becomes public. Again, the reason for their behavior is that the status of a rape victim is ambiguous.[5] A raped woman is not "clean." If a raped woman is married, her status as the property of one man is altered; at the time of rape she became the property of another man. This means that now she "belongs" to neither. Moreover, a rape victim is very often portrayed as responsible for the crime ("She was asking for it"). And what, if not ambiguous, is the status of a person who is responsible for a crime and is its victim at the same time?

> While men successfully convinced each other and us that women cry rape with ease and glee, the reality of rape is that victimized women have always been reluctant to report the crime and seek legal justice—because of the shame of public exposure, because of that complex double standard that makes a female feel culpable, even responsible, for any act of sexual aggression committed against her, because of possible retribution from the assailant (once a woman has been raped, the threat of a return engagement understandably looms large), and because women have been presented with sufficient evidence to come to the realistic conclusion that their accounts are received with a harsh cynicism that forms the first line of male defense. (Brownmiller, 1975, pp. 434-435)

Speaking about the sources of women's silence in the wider context of women's oppression, Cameron (1985a) concentrates mainly on the negative stereotyping of women and its multifaceted consequences. Women are said not to use language but "women's language." No matter whether it is only an imagined quality of women's communicating style or whether it is an empirically verifiable style, its assumed or true existence commonly leads to the treatment of females as *inadequate communicators.* Having the status of an inadequate communicator within one's own speech community definitely puts one in an unclear position. Indeed, as in the other cases discussed so far, the predictable outcome of such ambiguity is the silence of women. Cameron notes that the silence of females is prescribed for them by force of folk-linguistic value judgments (encoded, for example, in etiquette books), and controlled by more or less institutionalized means (e.g., in periods of silence enforced on women due to participation in various ritualized activities).

Cameron points out another reason for women's silence in Western societies: Females have traditionally defined and symbolized the private domain as opposed to the public. When they appeared in the latter, their status was perceived as marginal or, as I would like to call it once again, abnormal-ambiguous. Therefore, not many female voices have been heard in the public domain or in areas involving the use of ritual speech. Following Kaplan, Cameron observes that women are treated as if they were children: Both groups are to be seen and not heard.

Other authors have discussed how women's silence has had to be overcome on a macro level of social struggle. An important way for women activists to be heard by the public in a mass-media-oriented society like the United States was to reach the media. Amundsen (1981) states that the U.S. male-controlled media were not willing to give time and space for the women's movement to speak out, in the same manner as the same, white-controlled media would not let black activists of the 1950s and the 1960s voice their arguments against racial oppression.

As has been said above, silenced groups, in principle, are deprived of any official means of expression. Reaching the intended audience has to take various unconventional forms often bordering on what is declared by the dominant group as criminal activity (e.g., underground publications, rallies organized without the permission of the authorities, graffiti). Amundsen shows that even if an oppressed group (here women) gained access to the official media it was also accomplished in unconventional ways.

> A shortcut had to be found. It was the same for the civil rights movement as for the antiwar movement a few years later: Political demonstrations, boycotts, sit-ins, civil disobedience—every tactic still available to "out-groups" in the political system had to be used. The catchword was *news*. To get the attention of the media, it was not enough to be right, to be moral, to be responsible; one had to be, above all, *news-worthy*. And one becomes news-worthy if the issue is raised dramatically, if the challenge is posed vividly, if one's cause is demonstrated boldly. That is something no mass media in a free society can resist. Where requests to cover meetings and speeches or to broadcast messages for reformist and radical activists will fall on the very dead ears of status-quo-oriented editors and news chiefs, the confrontations initiated by activists contain too much drama, too much portent for change to be ignored. (Amundsen, 1981, pp. 171-172)[6]

The above assessment of women's subordination and their uncertain position both in public and private domains has corroborated my claim based on Leach's theory that dominated groups whose status is that of abnormality-ambiguity are silenced. Members of such groups often feel anxiety and experience conflict with self-identification (cf. Walkerdine, 1985) or, in other words, self-expression. They can be characterized as being in a schizophrenic (Sennet & Cobb, 1972), or in a double-bind situation (Bateson, 1972). When the feeling of one's ambivalence in relation to the accepted norms or values of the outside world prevail, the resulting state is silence. When the dominated group feels that it can no longer accept its abnormal status and subordination, it begins a fight for its right to speak. The following section gives an example of such a struggle.

4.5.4 Solidarity Trade Union

Free access to the mass media was a great concern for the Solidarity trade union in Poland during the 16 months of its first official existence between August 1980 and December 1981. Of course, Solidarity was newsworthy but little unbiased and reliable reporting on the union reached mass circulated, state-controlled media: the daily newspapers, radio, and television. *Tygodnik Solidarnosc* ("Solidarity Weekly"), whose 37 issues were published in the official circulation system between April 3 and December 11, 1981, documented the inaccessibility of the union to the media and the union's overall unsuccessful struggle to reach the public.

A close look at *Tygodnik Solidarnosc* (published in 1980-1981) materials dealing with the union's access to the media (or the lack of it), the workings of censorship at that time, and the union's efforts to gain the right to speak with its own voice reveals a broad range of silencing techniques in politics. The following are just some of the relevant examples.

Important events in Solidarity's life, such as the congress of Rural Solidarity, were not at all mentioned in the official press. Certainly a prototypical case of *przemilczenie* ("failing to mention something"). Other events, such as the Bydgoszcz case,[7] were reported in a clearly biased manner accompanied by altering of the facts. Although a lot of materials were published about Solidarity, few publications were allowed to present the union's own, self-articulated position on various matters. For example, one day the publication of the daily *Wieczór Wroclawia* ("The Wroclaw Evening") was delayed for a few hours because censorship banned part of the story on the Bydgoszcz case, in which the local (Wroclaw) chapter of Solidarity expressed its own opinion on what had happened. In place of printed information there was a white space on the page. Interestingly, the printers retaliated against this silencing measure in kind by refusing to print the official account of the events provided by the state-controlled Polish Press Agency. Eventually, the paper appeared with two white spaces instead of one.

Almost 1 year passed from the time of Solidarity's birth before the union managed to finalize its negotiations with the government concerning its access to the official media, mainly television and radio. However, the agreement never came to be respected by the government. Solidarity remained absent from the media, and its views continued to be presented in a distorted manner. The leaders of the then Association of Polish Journalists called the media's continuous attacks on Solidarity without the union's right to respond to them "a disinformation campaign."

It was of great concern for the union to be able to receive fair radio and television coverage of its first National Congress in Gdansk in September 1981. The terms offered by the government did not satisfy the union because they did not guarantee unbiased reporting and the union's control of the aired statements. In response to that, Polish Radio and Television were unaccredited to the congress. Other means of informing the public about the congress had to be found. One way was to double the circulation of the relatively free weekly *Tygodnik Solidarnosc* to a million copies. Also, an independent Solidarity video crew documented the congress.

As has been stated (§4.4.5), an oppressed group can break its silence by choosing media of communication that are not controlled by the power group. A rather obvious way for the union to respond to its silencing was to silence the official press in return, and a printers' strike—known as "the days without the press,"—was conducted on August 19 and 20, 1981. Alternative ways of reaching the public were also sought. One of the most effective ones proved to be the widespread use of films made by the union's own production teams and shown widely outside the official distribution system (mainly in churches).

The union published its own information bulletins and posters, which were put up on walls practically everywhere. Both these media for spreading information were confronted with silencing measures: The posters were torn down, and the people who distributed the union printed matter were threatened and instructed not to continue such work.

Just as Solidarity was silenced on important public matters, it was also denied the right to be silent (cf. O'Barr, 1982; Rice, 1961) when it desired. On at least one occasion, the official press and radio published without permission transcripts and recordings from a closed session of Solidarity's leadership in the town of Radom. Needless to say, the published material was tailored to suit the needs of the official propaganda. *Tygodnik Solidarnosc*, which called this event "A Polish Watergate," complained that every organization has a right to closed conferences and under no circumstances should that right be violated.

4.5.5 Silencing Political Opposition: Some More Examples

The silencing of political opposition or other oppressed groups is not limited to only one or two local regimes or conservative leaders. The phenomenon discussed here is present almost universally where power struggle is involved, and it can be called the *tabooing* of a group to impose silence on it. Then even speaking about such a group constitutes a crime. The reader will recall Leach's (1982) assertion quoted above that, within his framework of analyzing culture, "the essence of sin is disobedience to a taboo" (p. 115).

After the brutal suppression of the peaceful student demonstrations in Tiananmen Square in Beijing on June 4, 1989, official Chinese propaganda described the students and their actions using overtly undesirable, derogatory terms. At the same time, the students were not referred to as "students," which established their ambiguous status and in consequence led to their silencing.

When the Chinese army attacked the demonstrators in Tiananmen Square it was said in the official radio news bulletin to have suppressed a "counterrevolutionary riot" (or counterrevolutionary chaos or counterrevolutionary rebellion). This meant that the students were not peaceful and not in favor of any positive changes but were violent and destructive. The only casualties mentioned in the first days were among the troops (thus the students became killers or criminals). An information leakage occurred when one announcer on the English-language broadcast of Radio Beijing spoke of many thousand innocent civilian casualties, but silence was promptly restored by the authorities who banned further broadcasting of the program (cf. *The Times*, 1989a, p. 1).

Another move of propaganda was to publish the Chinese Communist party's Central Committee's "Letter to the People," which praised great numbers of people including progovernment students who supported the army's victory over the "rebels" (cf. *The Times*, 1989b, p. 2). This strategy renders the student demonstrators ambiguous by claiming that they were practically isolated from (when, in fact, they were greatly supported by) most of their fellow students and the people of Beijing.

As this example demonstrates, creating a feeling of ambiguity and ambivalence around a dominated or opposition group may help the socially, economically, and politically dominant groups create silence around the oppressed. It is easier to conceal the truth and deceive the public about what is going on when the events in question are the responsibility of some unimportant or devalued individuals (hooligans, unbalanced people, rioters, etc.) whose status is unclear, rather than a clearly defined dominated group with accepted rights and status. A *Newsweek* report quotes the then Czechoslovak leader, Milos Jakes

> that *he* has no patience for independent voices. "Extending democracy in no way means making room for the legalization of political opposition which, as all experience so far has shown, cannot but be anti-socialist." ("Activating the Activists," 1988, p. 38)

Obviously, the legalization of an opposition group would not make it more or less antisocialist. What is at stake here is the government's continuing possibility of disregarding whoever is a threat to the status quo when their status is ambiguous, as is clearly the case with underground political opposition groups.

Manipulation of this kind is largely intentional and is aimed at deceiving the public. After the price strikes in June 1976 in the towns of Radom and Ursus in Poland, the leading weekly, *Polityka*, attempted to report the events in a way that turned out to be unacceptable to the authorities. The original text was altered, and a memo to all the censors explained:

> [because] the . . . text leads the reader to assume that only Walter [a production plant in Radom] employees took part in the incidents, the editors, acting on our suggestion, supplemented the text by noting the participation of "parasitic elements, ruffians, criminals and anti-socialist elements." ("Informative note," 1984, pp. 105-106)

Of course, if it had been admitted that the workers and no one else had gone on strike, the authorities (in a workers' state) would probably have had to take a clear position on the issue. However, because the unrest was the responsibility of "parasitic elements, ruffians, criminals and antisocialist elements," there was no need to talk to the strikers or about the strikes themselves.

In a more recent wave of strikes in Poland in August 1988, the strikes were declared illegal by the then authorities. The organizers and participants of the strikes became law breakers and suspects. When there was some mention of the organizers of the strikes, the media focused on the people (opposition members) who aided and joined the strikes from outside the workplaces involved in the actions. In this way, the organizers of the strikes were categorized principally as nonworkers, as well as the real enemies of the working class or egotistical dissidents.

When the political situation begins to slip out from the control of the power group, and the opposition starts to voice protests against the existing political situation, extreme silencing measures are often applied. One tragic group of brutally silenced people are the "missing people" in a number of Latin American countries.

In her fascinating article on the formation of "intertextual relationships" in a series of texts dealing with *desaparecidos*, "missing people" in Argentina, Lavandera (1986) describes ways of manipulating language to produce an effect that supports my present argument. In 1983, the military government in Argentina published a document with the purpose of accounting before the public for the *desaparecidos*—political opponents of the government who had been known to be detained in prisons and concentration camps, and tortured or executed. The document came to be known as the "Final Document." It was the first time the military government was to publicly acknowledge that there were missing people in Argentina. However, as Lavandera shows in her analysis, having manipulated the language in a certain way, the government did not really acknowledge anything. Here, I will mention only the part of her study that deals with the use of key lexical entries in the Final Document.

The main lexical entries of the text are: *desaparecidos* ("missing people"), *terrorismo* ("terrorism"), *represion* ("repression"), and *subversion* ("subversion"). The status of *desaparecidos* is changed and becomes ambiguous by equating the subversive actions of the missing people with terrorist acts. Thus "all subversives are terrorists" (Lavandera, 1986, p. 127). Furthermore, the meaning of the term *desaparecidos*, used significantly less frequently than the prominent *terrorismo*, is changed so that in the Final Document it refers to all the dirty war casualties, civilian *and* military.

Once a group's status is established as ambiguous, genuine discussion of its existence is neither possible nor necessary. Such was also the case with the *desaparecidos* mentioned in the Final Document. The other documents published in Argentina as a reaction to the Final Document followed suit and did not go beyond its original rhetoric. This is a sad example of double silencing. First, a group of individuals is kidnapped and there is no record of their tragic fate, and then their existence is tabooed so that no genuine talk about them is possible.[8]

4.5.6 Silenced Individuals

The ambiguous status of individuals, and the silence resulting from this can also be encountered on the interpersonal level. For example, recently divorced spouses, babies born with certain genetic defects, and deceased members of one's family are subject to greater or lesser taboo. Mention of such individuals in casual, social conversations is avoided.

Bruneau (1973) recognizes this type of silence as a reaction to diversity. A silent response may be a sign of rejection of physical, psychological, or verbal diversity. The perception of someone's *otherness* will, of course, depend on one's stereotypes and prejudices. The more different another person appears to be from one's self, the more profound will be the silence of puzzlement, embarrassment, or anticipation of disambiguation of the situation. The burden of such disambiguation lies with the person perceived as deviant in relation to the mainstream norm.

Fat persons, dwarfs, very tall persons, crippled persons with mobility problems, blind persons, persons with pronounced speech or hearing disorders, etc., have known nervous silences toward them. Differences in appearance, such as perceived ugliness, dress, and color of skin, when different than the situational norm, seem to be greeted by initial silences. The strength of these silences seems to depend on the uniqueness of the difference of the observer. (Bruneau, 1973, p. 32).

The simplest and the most common example of a person with an ambiguous status who needs to break the situational silence, and in this way to disambiguate his or her status is that of a stranger or intruder. A newcomer to a territory has to start a verbal exchange with those who are already present. In this way he or she can negotiate the use of the territory that is already occupied by others. Other things being equal, the stranger or intruder always has a lower status than others (clear exceptions are highly stratified, institutionalized hierarchies, like the military). Consider two Polish examples: When one travels on a train, and like everyone else has a ticket and a reserved seat, coming into a compartment where other passengers have already taken their seats requires the newly arrived person to offer the initial greeting formula. The person who comes into the waiting room of a doctor's office greets others first, rather than vice versa. These rather trivial examples support the point that it is the transitional, uncertain, ambiguous moment of one's becoming "one of us" rather than remaining "one of them," that requires his or her initial verbal move. It is also by speaking to a stranger or intruder that others indicate their willingness to accept him or her as part of their group. The right to speak may be granted implicitly, for example, when the newcomer is asked a question, or it may be granted explicitly. For example, when on one occasion I audited a linguistics class, the professor, having introduced me to the students, said to me: "Feel free to take part in the discussion." Granting me a right to speak (to break my silence), she indicated that on that particular occasion I was recognized as a regular member of the classroom community.

4.6 Conclusion

In this chapter I documented how silence works and is used in various aspects of political and social life. It has been shown that some functions of speech and silence merge when they are analyzed within a common theoretical framework. Although silence is usually associated with the absence of communication (cf. Chapter 2), it turns out that in political discourse some forms of silence are capable of producing contextual effects (in terms of the theory of relevance) that its use is indeed very effective (cf. §§4.4.1 and 4.4.2). On the other hand, the use of words need not be always connected with effective communication. For example, the contextual effects, and hence relevance, of some advertisements may be minimal because of frequent repetition of a given ad or the existence of another one, conflicting with the message of the first. This is not to say that silence in politics should always be perceived in positive terms. As a matter of fact, this chapter has focused on the opposite valuation of silence. It has identified several forms of silence and silencing measures the primary functions of which were to withhold relevant information, and exert control over politically and socially dominated groups. An attempt has been made to frame most of the discussion of the oppressive silence in Leach's cultural anthropological theory. The main point was to show that silencing a group (or an individual) through creating and maintaining their ambiguous status is deliberate and forms an inseparable part of every power struggle.

Restating the essence of my argument in more abstract terms, I would like to draw an analogy between Walkerdine's (1985) notion of a person's ability to negotiate the boundaries of his or her identity and Leach's (1964) idea of negotiating the ambiguous boundaries with reference to one's body. Children have to learn the limits of their bodies. They have to realize what belongs to them and what does not. These boundaries are seldom clear. Therefore, once the physiological products of one's body (urine, feces, menstrual blood, semen, nail clippings, etc.) leave their natural environment (i.e., the body), they immediately become a taboo. At the same time they are and they are not one's body. Likewise, the boundaries of our social and psychological limits (self-identity) are fuzzy. Members of various minority and dominated groups, for example, feel ambivalent and distressed when they face problems of self-identification. In his theory, Leach discusses the crossing of physical (physiological) and social boundaries. Walkerdine concentrates on the significance of overcoming psychological boundaries. In each case, the person characterized by an ambiguous status becomes a taboo and his or her expected state is that of silence.

As has become apparent, I have treated the term *politics* in a very general sense. Likewise, the concept of *silence* has been exploited in a way that points to its multifaceted nature: taking various forms and performing numerous functions. The next chapter will deal with the use of silence in the arts. The concepts *silence* and *arts* will both, again, be treated as very broad categories.

Notes

1. It seems reasonable to restrict Moran's distinction between the two types of language use to *macro contexts,* such as scientific language, genuine political discourse, and reliable commercial information (communication), and political propaganda and advertising (pseudocommunication). It is also necessary to bear in mind that not all authors would restrict the term *communication* so that advertising would not belong to it. For example, Vestergaard and Schroder (1985) state that "advertising is of course a form of communication." It is "verbal/nonverbal, public, one-way communication" (p. 13).

2. This type of silence should not be understood as strategic in Brummett's (1980) sense, because it was announced by Carter beforehand and thus was expected by everyone.

3. It is interesting to note that once the unofficial way of transmitting information to the public is legalized it may lose its appeal for the oppressed group and be abandoned. For example, in early summer of 1989 the municipal authorities of Wroclaw had two large, white boards constructed in the city center for anyone to write whatever they wanted on them. This was designed to save many building walls from the proliferating political graffiti and thus to reduce the cost of cleaning up the city. However, the official boards did not gain the appeal of the political graffiti writers and the texts appearing on the boards became mainly personal in nature ("I love Jola," "Beata is a whore") (Wawak, 1989, p. 4).

4. Zimmerman and West's research has been challenged by Murray (see Murray, 1985, 1987; Murray & Covelli, 1988). He claims that interrupting is not a gender-related variable, but that it belongs to the verbal repertoire of both middle-class men and women. In his own empirical work (Murray & Covelli, 1988), Murray shows that women can, at times, interrupt men more than vice versa. Furthermore, interruption, like all other linguistic forms is plurifunctional and cannot always be interpreted negatively. On the one hand, interruption may indeed indicate aggressive domination, but it may also show concern for the interrupted person (e.g., interrupting one's apology), or support (when giving short comments of agreement with what the other party is saying) (see also Bennett, 1981). It has to be noted, however, that these solitary functions of interruption are more likely to appear in women's speech, which is marked by higher involvement (*rapport-talk*) than in the speech of men, for whom conversation is more of a competing game (*report-talk*), where fighting for the floor is more common than sharing it (cf. Tannen, 1990).

5. Leach (1977) also states that in most Western legal systems sexual offenses are not recognized as the most prototypical crimes (such as homicide or theft, for example).

6. Indeed, when someone is not newsworthy, the media will not take any interest in what a given person or group may have to say. Such public silencing during the 1988 presidential primary campaigns in the United States was the fate of Democratic candidate Gary Hart after his big loss in the Iowa caucus. Before that, Hart had been followed everywhere by numerous reporters. However, losing political support also meant an abrupt loss of Hart's opportunities to speak out publicly and

be recorded as so speaking.

> Sitting with a few aides in a nearly deserted Manchester [New Hampshire] restaurant, Hart watched his hastily resurrected campaign absorb another death blow, this time at the hands of the people he was counting on to save it: the voters. A few reporters dropped by, but left as the extent of Hart's decline became apparent. When Hart went to the nearby CBS studio for a prearranged interview, the producers politely told him they weren't interested anymore. The networks had no time for a candidate who could garner only 1 percent of the vote in Iowa. . . .
>
> Last week, as Hart campaigned at the Nashua Boys Club, a few journalists tagged along but left early. Hart remained on the basketball court, shooting hoops with a group of kids. While other candidates were out hustling votes, Hart kept playing—a man with a message but without an audience. ("Hart," 1988, p. 233)

7. On April 19, 1981, the police interrupted and terminated a meeting between the Bydgoszcz Region Council and the Bydgoszcz chapter of Solidarity. Several Solidarity members were severely beaten by the police.

8. Where the right to impose silence is a desirable means of displaying one's power and authority (and this may be a very common practice across cultures) the recognition of the advantages following from being able to do so are learned early on in life. In their book on the language of English schoolchildren Opie and Opie (1959) state, "If a child has no authority for obtaining quiet he can seek it by brute force, by verbal force, or by guile. Verbal force can be very effective" (p. 214). The authors go on to list numerous imperatives ("Cut the cackle," "Dry up," "Put a cork in," etc.) and guile ("The first person to speak after me is a monkey" [ape, ass, donkey, etc.], "Silence in the pig market, the fat pig wants to speak," etc.), all of which are said to be very powerful silencers.

CHAPTER FIVE

The Extensions of Silence

5.1 Introduction

The title of this chapter makes an obvious reference to the famous book by Marshall McLuhan (1974) *Understanding Media: The Extensions of Man.* I am going to discuss here some phenomena from outside language, but in relation to the linguistic aspects of silence. I will deal mainly with certain forms of artistic expression in visual arts, although they could be easily extended to literature and music. I do not claim any exhaustiveness in discussing these matters. However, I believe that the theoretical foundations for the study of silence developed in the earlier chapters can be well adapted for the analysis of some aspects of artistic expression, especially if one wants, and I do, to see art as a medium of communication.

Obviously, the base of all my considerations lies in language, and also here I will largely rely on certain concepts and ideas developed and exploited in relation to the study of language. For example, I will refer to *frame analysis* (Goffman, 1974; Tannen, 1979). First, however, let us once again take a look at silence itself as a *medium* of communication.

McLuhan (1974) divides media into two kinds—*hot* and *cool:*

> there is a basic principle that distinguishes a hot medium like radio from a cool one like the telephone, or a hot medium like the movie from a cool one like TV. A hot medium is one that extends one single sense in "high definition." High definition is the state of being well filled with data. A photograph is, visually, "high definition." A

> cartoon is "low definition," simply because very little visual information is provided. Telephone is a cool medium, or one of low definition, because the ear is given a meager amount of information. And speech is a cool medium of low definition, because so little is given and so much has to be filled in by the listener. On the other hand, hot media do not leave so much to be filled in or completed by the audience. Hot media are, therefore, low in participation or completion by the audience. Naturally, therefore, a hot medium like radio has very different effects on the user from a cool medium like the telephone. (p. 36)

If speech is a relatively cool medium, then silence must be even cooler. That is probably why silence is generally not considered to be a suitable medium of communication, although whether and to what degree this is the case is an interesting empirical question worth investigating in the future. Admittedly, communicating in silence may require from the participants more filling in, more completion, and higher participation than communicating in speech. From this standpoint, and it is not incompatible with my analysis of silence in the light of Sperber and Wilson's (1986) relevance theory, silence is a medium of communication whose processing requires more cognitive effort than speech.

5.2. Silence and the Artistic Tradition of the West

As far as the artistic tradition of the West is concerned silence is not commonly regarded as a positive means of communication and/or expression. This is well reflected in Steiner's (1976) confusing, although rather influential, essay "The Retreat from the Word," in which the author discusses some aspects of 20th-century intellectual and artistic development.

Those forms and phenomena that do not appeal to him or that he feels contain no "messages" are, according to Steiner, instances of modern humans "retreating from the word"—falling into silence. In other words, the only meaningful linguistic forms are those concerning speech and writing, and the only meaningful experience is that which can be verbalized. Consider two excerpts from the essay in which Steiner (1976) equates meaninglessness in modern art with silence in language:

> The abstract design conveys only the rudimentary pleasures of decoration. Much of Jackson Pollock is vivid wallpaper. And in the majority of cases, abstract expressionism and non-objective art communicate nothing whatever. The work stands mute or attempts to shout at us in a kind of inhuman gibberish. I wonder whether future artists and critics will not look back with puzzled contempt upon the mass of pretentious trivia that now fills our galleries. (p. 43)

And:

> Modern music . . . denies him [the listener] any recognition of content, or, more accurately, it denies him the possibility of relating the purely auditive impression to any verbalized form of experience. (p. 43)

Steiner expresses the idea that abstract art is meaningless and that meaninglessness is a function of silence. Later in this chapter I am going to argue to the contrary that silence in visual arts exists on different levels and that it is meaningful, it takes various forms, and performs different functions. Of course, silence in visual arts should be understood as an *extension* of linguistic silence, of which the most prototypical case is that of absence of speech. In visual terms, the most prototypical examples of silence will involve instances of paintings with minimal internal contrast. Before developing my argument, however, let us look again at Steiner's essay and point out a general inconsistency present in it.

At the beginning, Steiner (1976) observes that it is not necessarily a human universal always to relate to verbal experience. He gives examples of Buddhism and Taoism in which

> the highest, purest reach of the contemplative act is that which has learned to leave language behind it. The ineffable lies beyond the frontiers of the word. It is only by breaking through the walls of language that visionary observance can enter the world of total and immediate understanding. Where such understanding is attained, the truth need no longer suffer the impurities and fragmentation that speech necessarily entails. (p. 31)

Steiner observes, indeed as several other authors do (§§2.5.3 and 2.6.1), that in the Western tradition silence is valued very differently than in many non-Western cultures.

> Pascal is nearer the mainstream of classic Western feeling when he says that the silence of cosmic space strikes terror. To the Taoist that selfsame silence conveys tranquillity and the intimation of God. (p. 32)

But despite his recognition of the differences in the valuation of silence in the East and West, Steiner is unable to apply his understanding of the communicative powers of silence to his analysis of modern art in the West. First, silence is referred to as facilitating understanding and freeing from the rigid confines of speech (East), and then it is dismissed as meaningless (West).

My interpretation of modern art takes a radically different view, in which silence is one of the key concepts making this art meaningful. In fact, much of the meaningful and meditative silence present in today's art comes from the great influence of Eastern philosophy on Western philosophy and art in the 1960s.

An abstract painting does go beyond verbal experience in many ways, and contemplating it does not necessarily require verbalization of any kind. Instead of seeing this as a weakness of abstract painting, one should see it as its strength. A lot of poetry, apparently the most verbal art form, is very powerful because of what is left unsaid, as in *haiku,* for example. Most classical music exists without a program and does not really need it to be appreciated. Likewise, when Cage (1961) articulates his doctrine of experimental music he argues against any necessary *purpose* or *theme* in music, which for him is just *sounds* (pp. 13-17).

On the other hand I am against the simplistic treatment of silence in painting that states that all painting is to some degree silent. For example, Fibichner (1982) argues that silence is a profound element in painting because it is present in both the creative process of painting and contemplating it in the museum. Besides, silence is evoked by the painting's harmonious composition and geometric construction, use of color (especially blue), theme (especially still-life), degree of abstraction (any abstraction), reference to transcendental or infinite objects of nature (e.g., clouds, sea, mountains), medium (especially watercolor), the transparency of the colors (white paper equals areas of silence), and size (especially large). Some silences associated with paintings are meditative and religious, others express incomprehensibility of an artwork. And one of the opening statements of Fibichner's (1982) essay is "Silence surrounds painting" (p. 13). Such an approach to silence in painting cannot be accepted here. I find it rather uninformative and even confusing. The main problem that I see with Fibichner's approach is its atheoretical view of silence. Silence for him means many things: a psychological experience (meditation, contemplation); a linguistic expression of transcendence, sacredness, or incomprehensibility; and a formal property of the visual plane (stillness). The author discusses the silence of the painter, the viewer, the painting itself, or the space in which it is perceived. On the one hand, Fibichner (1982) uses the metaphor "art is [a] language" and states that "one can 'read' a picture" (p. 13), but when he discusses the silent paintings of Vermeer he concludes that "there is an almost total lack of story-telling. Vermeer's women are pure visual phenomena, utterly self-sufficient, needing no anecdotal element and no comment. Since the painter is only concerned with what is visible, words become useless" (p. 14). To me this passage suggests that artistic language is associated only with the verbal in natural languages (cf. Steiner quoted above) and that Vermeer's resorting to silence is not any longer linguistic or communicative.

As can be seen from the above, in order not to confuse the possible meanings and forms of silence, one must choose a theoretical framework that will specify the understanding of the concept and will provide further analytic tools for making relevant generalizations. This will also prevent us from making some indiscriminate and trivial claims like: All painting is silent.

5.3 Frame Analysis

According to the theory of frame analysis (Goffman, 1974), social and natural situations can be interpreted on various levels. For example, telling a story will be interpreted differently depending on whether it is recognized as an account of real-life events, as joking, or as a theatrical monologue. Events may have a multi-leveled structure with respect to the framing processes, as in Shakespeare's use of the play within a play in *Hamlet*. The multi-layering of events in this scene is truly remarkable. First, there is the story of Gonzago's murder framed in a theatrical production. To the audience on stage this should not appear as anything else but a play. But Hamlet's manipulative choice of the text for the play turns it into a fabrication to attack the king. All this is happening as part of the play written by Shakespeare, in which the staged audience are really actors before a real audience.

> So one has, starting from the innermost point, a strip of events that could have actually occurred, transformed for dramatic production, retransformed as a construction to entrap the King, transformed once again, since all this plotting actually happens in a play, not merely by means of a play. And of course, the mountain of literary comment on the play is a keying of all this. (Goffman, 1974, p. 184)

Our next step in the study of silence will be to combine frame analysis with another interpretive framework referred to in an earlier chapter, namely the theory of metaphors (§3.5.1).

5.3.1 Applying Frame Analysis to the Study of Silence

The concept of *framing* is capable of explaining different uses of silence for various purposes. Dauenhauer (1980) mentions all kinds of silence in relation to sound—for example, to words and music—and in relation to human activities that do not involve any sound—for example, performing arts based on gestures and disciplined movements (mime), private reading, painting, and sculpture. The author claims further that silence can exist without sound, arguing that deaf individuals experience silence and also that when one is distracted from an activity that requires silence (reading or viewing a work of art) the silence that is necessary for carrying out these activities will be perceived as absent.

I think it is important, however, to make a functional distinction among these types of silence to understand how they are experienced in different situations and what functions they perform.

Differentiating among various kinds of silence in relation to sounds and activities will here be a function of applying frame analysis as a theoretical grid for studying silence.

For example, take the silence that occurs during a theatrical performance of a play and the silence of a pantomime show. In the former case the audience's expectations of the occurring silence(s) will be different from those in the latter case. In a theater play, silence is recognized to have communicative value (contextual effects) for the story or for the emotional involvement of the characters. Silence is an integral part of the script (or the stage production), which is all framed by the convention of the performance. And I am disregarding here an actor's silence caused by his or her forgetting the words of the play. This silence belongs to yet another frame: the frame of professionals (actors) doing their job and a group of consumers (audience) partaking of the product (performance) of their work (acting). Onstage mixing of silences, and in fact, any other attributes belonging to different frames, may indeed yield comical or embarrassing results.

The silence of mimes, on the other hand, does not offer any additional meaning to the plot of the performance. It is actually the silence (i.e., absence of actors' words, but not necessarily lack of music or other sounds such as heavy breathing, noise of falling objects, etc.) that frames the acting, recognized by the audience as pantomime.

These two types of silence can be accounted for by Lakoff and Johnson's (1980) theory of metaphors referred to in §3.5.1. To restate their position briefly: Activities are conceptualized metaphorically as substances, and states as containers. The first of the two types of silence discussed above (i.e., actors' silence in a play) can be conceptualized as an activity that finds its metaphorical extension in treating it (silence) as a *substance.* Just like in a real-life conversation, actors' silence fills in the setting of their interaction, creating, for example, *walls* over which they cannot communicate, or *platforms* of mutual understanding. Silent moments, just like words, take shape within the frame of a staged play.

The silence of the pantomime, on the other hand, is not viewed here as an activity of the actors, but rather as a state in which their performance takes place. Therefore, we can metaphorically speak about the pantomime silence as a *container* that provides a wider frame for the viewing of a show.

The functional distinction between "framed" and "framing" silences has been thus justified by showing how this simple taxonomy constitutes a function of a more general framework: a cognitive theory of metaphors. An analogous view of silence can now be extended to the visual medium.

5.3.2 Frame Analysis, Silence, and Painting

The silence that is said to be present in much of Japanese painting (cf. §5.3.4) frames, or provides a level of interpretation for, the image depicted in the painting: a flower, tree, mountain, bird, or monkey. This silence, in turn, becomes an integral part of the image when we look at it through the frame of the entire picture, and apart from interpreting the meaning (or significance or simply the beauty) of the flower, tree, mountain, bird, or monkey, we can also appreciate the meaning (significance, beauty) of what is left out, the apparently blank spaces on paper. Finally, there is the silence framing the painting and the viewer together: the silence of contemplation.

The appropriateness of using frame analysis for uncovering and discussing different layers of meaning in painting follows from the origin of the concept. Tannen informs us that the term *frame* was originally used by Bateson in 1955 "to explain how individuals exchange signals that allow them to agree upon the level of abstraction at which any message is intended" (Tannen, 1979, p. 141). And indeed the physical analogy of a picture frame was the one Bateson (1972, p. 186) used to account for his use of this notion in a psychological context.

Traditionally, a painting is a physical object. Usually, it takes the form of a canvas, wooden panel, metal plate, or some other flat surface on which a pattern of paint and/or another medium has been arranged. The boundaries of paintings are clear. Nevertheless, most paintings, as they are seen in galleries and museums, are more or less elaborately framed. There is of course an aesthetic reason for framing paintings, especially when the frame itself is a work of art or craftsmanship. But it is also possible to look at the frame in a functional perspective. Namely, the frame emphasizes the separation of the painting from reality. The painted canvas is an "illusion" that needs separation from the "real."

In most representational art, viewers look for a "plot" (cf. Fibichner, 1982; Steiner, 1976). A painting is supposed to tell us something. It can be a story, a myth, a tale, an anecdote, a transposition of the painter's feelings and emotions about a political issue (e.g., revolution), a religious event (e.g., a biblical story), and so on. A portrait tells us something about the model. A surrealist painting has the task of narrating the painter's dream. In all these cases the painting is related to the verbal.[1] Silence in painting is associated with nothingness and nihilism, i.e., Dada.

There is a level then where Steiner's (1976) idea that there is a connection between verbalization in art and its meaningfulness gains support. We interpret a given painting as if it were a theatrical play. Of course, the story is accepted as real only as much as it is confined to its own frame. Outside of its frame, the picture loses its force as a performance and becomes an image, an illustration, a formal arrangement of shapes and/or colors, a decorative object hung on the wall, or an investment. Apart from the decorative function, a picture may express or reinforce certain values of its owner (e.g., a religious painting) or it may indicate the taste or display the wealth of the owner. Whatever the function of the painting as object may be, to see it one has to step outside of the painting's own frame. The painting's story is accessible to the viewer only when it is looked at within the frame.

With respect to silence, one can find it takes on different forms, depending on the formal properties of paintings and the framing processes involved in their interpretation. Recall that the term *frame* is used here "to explain how individuals exchange signals that allow them to agree upon the level of abstraction at which any message is intended" (Tannen, 1979, p. 141). Therefore, Steiner's (1976) interpretation of the painting on only one, literary, or verbal, level has to be rejected because it does not allow for the flexibility of *transforming* and *keying* (both Goffman's terms) the framing process. If painters and viewers are allowed to decide for themselves to what degree abstraction is present in a given work of art, then the intended and received messages encoded and decoded in a painting will not have to be confined to their verbal experience.

5.3.3 Hopper's Silence

Silence can, of course, be present in the stories told in representative (figurative) paintings. This is the level of Steiner's interpretation. The American painter Edward Hopper, for example, is known for his silent landscapes of rural and urban America. Many of his paintings are depictions of American architecture: typical, seemingly unattractive, buildings set in motionless landscapes, often deprived of people hidden behind closed windows (e.g., *Early Sunday Morning,* 1930). When people appear in Hopper's paintings they are very often still, almost stiff, and looking blindly ahead. Even when Hopper shows us people who talk to each other, there is no way we can "hear" them and find out what they are talking about, as if we were looking at these people on television in slow motion and with the volume turned off (e.g., *Nighthawks,* 1942; *Chop Suey,* 1929). In one of the paintings (*Four Lane Road,* 1956) a woman is shown shouting at a man, but he does not seem to hear her, or the shouting of the woman has no impact on him. As O'Doherty (n.d.) states in his film on Hopper's painting: "The only shout in Hopper's work still hasn't reached who it was meant for."

The silence of Hopper's paintings forms part of the stories that they relate; it is the narrative silence. The stories are about the loneliness, isolation, and depression of Americans at a certain time in their history. But the more general theme that can be called on in the interpretation of these paintings is that of the universal experience of loneliness and isolation of any people (Richardson, 1956; Rose, 1977). Therefore, apart from the narrative silence of Hopper's paintings being just part of his stories, we can identify another layer of silence whose interpretation involves a greater degree of abstraction. This layer is framed in the viewer's general psychological experience of human condition and his or her understanding of what it implies to be lonely, isolated, or depressed. Thus the meaning of Hopper's silence will depend on the psychological framing imposed on it by a given viewer.

From a formal point of view, there are still more complex framing processes in Hopper's painting. For example, in a painting showing an ocean view through the door of a sunlit, empty, silent room, the silence of the room frames (provides contrast for) the view of the ocean. Somewhat like in Japanese art (see §5.3.4), the viewer has to grasp the void of the empty room before the ocean view can be appreciated.

The theme of many of Hopper's paintings is privacy (O'Doherty, n.d.). To see someone in a private situation, for example, a strange naked woman, one cannot be in one room with her, otherwise she will not be private any more. Therefore, Hopper needed some kind of framing of a given situation that would allow the viewer to remain unseen, yet to be able to witness this situation. How did Hopper achieve his goal? What did he use to get over his artistic observer's paradox?

> Windows. He once talked to me about seeing inside and outside at the same time. Well, that needs a window. There's a lot of looking in and looking out of windows. (O'Doherty, n.d.)

Painting the inside and the outside at the same time brings to mind our earlier discussion of ambiguity and silence based on Leach's work (§§2.6.2 and 4.5.1). According to Leach (1976) boundary zones and entities with ambiguous status (*p* and not-*p* at the same time) are sacred, abnormal, and subject to taboo. Transposing the last of these characteristics (taboo) into linguistic terms, we can say that transitional, or boundary, zones are characterized by silence (or formulaic speech, cf. §2.6.2). Hopper's paintings abound in such transitional, ambiguous, silent areas. Apart from the above-mentioned works showing the inside and the outside of a room (office, restaurant, etc.), there are many others in which Hopper places his subjects in various transitional locations: doorways, doorsteps, balconies, and porches. People are also shown in other shifting states and changing places: in hotel rooms providing temporary accommodation, during an intermission at the theater, while traveling, or when actors bow in front of an audience after a performance. One of the outcomes of this temporal and spatial vagueness captured in Hopper's paintings is the emanating silence.

At the end of his film, O'Doherty brings this subject up once again and presents it in a way totally congruous with our approach to the relation between ambiguity and silence:

> He [Hopper] spent a lot of time at Truro looking at an empty canvas on the easel thinking of what was to go on it. Now [at the time of the author's visit] there was a painting on it. It was called *Sun in an Empty Room*. . . .
>
> So he went to the easel and talked about two things so fundamental to his work that it was almost uncanny. He said he'd been trying to paint inside and outside at the same time. And then he asked: "How does an empty room look, when there's no one there to see it?" Inside and outside seen together. And being there and not being there at the same time. For me that picture sums up everything towards which his art reached. It's the closest he came to that void, that silence which is half process and half paralysis. (O'Doherty, n.d.)

The above discussion has shown that silence, which is primarily an acoustic category, can indeed be transposed into a visual medium. However, we have not by any means exhausted all the possible ways we can talk about the extensions of silence into the visual, although other examples may be more controversial. Before we proceed to analyze them, let us take a brief look at an artistic tradition that makes silence one of its basic modes of expression.

5.3.4 Silence in Japanese Art

In a vein similar to the silence of an empty room from which Hopper shows us his ocean view, the emptiness around abstract and figurative forms in Japanese art provides us with a point of reference for the interpretation and understanding of these forms. Painting for a Western audience, Hopper had to justify his silence by framing the view of the ocean, and therefore, he painted it as if the viewer were watching it from a silent and at the same time realistic place. The Japanese need no pretext to justify their silent framing of forms. For example, the carefully arranged rocks in Japanese stone gardens are set in a kind of negative space provided by the white sand around them.

> The vacant space of the [Ryōan-ji] garden, like silence, absorbs the mind, frees it of petty detail, and serves as a visual guide—a means for penetrating through the "realm of multitudes." (Petersen, 1960, p. 105)

Such meditative emptiness is characteristic of much Japanese Zen art. On the one hand, it allows framing the forms that it surrounds and thus makes them meaningful. On the other hand, because the process is reciprocal, the forms embedded in the emptiness provide it with the necessary contrast that enables the spectators to notice the silence.

> It is at this point that we come to one of the basic paradoxes of Buddhist thought: Only through form can we realize emptiness. Emptiness is thus considered not as a concept reached by the analytical process of reasoning, but as a statement of intuition or perception: "a fact of experience as much as the straightness of a bamboo and the redness of a flower." (Suzuki, 1938, p. 32)
>
> From this "fact of experience" is derived the principle of *sumi* painting. The blank sheet of paper is perceived only as paper, and remains as paper. Only by filling the paper does it become empty. Much in the same way the sound of the frog plopping into the still pond creates the silence in Basho's well-known *haiku*. The sound gives form to the silence—the emptiness. In the No play it is through voice and instrument that we are aware of profound silence; elaborately colorful costumes create simplicity and bareness; and in the dance, movement creates stillness, and stillness becomes movement. (Petersen, 1960, p. 107)

Petersen calls the Buddhist approach to this interrelationship between emptiness and form a *paradox,* but the paradox is only apparent here. What he expresses about the Zen treatment of form and void leads to the simple conclusion that in this tradition of thought neither of the two categories is absolute and that one cannot be defined without the other. Therefore, I will argue further that the meaningfulness of silence in visual arts (as probably in any art) depends foremost on finding appropriate contrasts to what appears as the void. The outcome of such an approach will depend on the framing processes that are applied—of what I, as a spectator, will expect to see and understand from the given painting.

> Structures of expectation make interpretation possible, but in the process they also reflect back on perception of the world to justify that interpretation. (Tannen, 1979, p. 144)

Of special interest here is so-called silent abstract painting: the monochrome, where the use of silence is that of an activity exercised by the artist rather than a state for analyzing the picture's story. Formally, monochrome painting relies on the concept of possible minimal contrast within its frame. Although, as has been already said, the analysis of such a painting's meaning involves framing processes, the silence itself does not, in its basic layer, form the framing for the painting itself; it is the artist's activity, which due to the metaphor theory (cf. §3.5.1) can be conceptualized as a substance.

5.3.5 Monochrome Painting

In this section, I am going to use further examples from the visual arts as illustrations of extensions of unprototypical modes of communicative behavior. I will begin, however, by returning to the problem of the impossibility of pinning down silence (and its extensions) as an absolute and objective category (cf. §2.5.2).

In contemporary abstract art the main tendency of extending silence into the visual medium is connected with the search for meaning beyond the material (Kuspit, 1986). In the original idea of the first abstract painter, Wassily Kandinsky, abstract art was to shift the attention of the art world from the material to the spiritual. The function of an abstract painting was to induce a kind of contemplative state comparable to religious experience.

Of course, the ability to evoke a meditative, silent state in the viewer contemplating a work of (visual) art cannot be limited to abstract art only. However, it is true that abstract art skips the verbal story present in representational painting and leads directly to the nonverbal, silent mode of expression and its perception. If, apart from the purely formal aspects of an abstract painting, there is no other way in which a viewer can relate to it, there will probably be little if any link established between the painting and the viewer. The intended spirituality of the painting will not affect the viewer. In other words, the viewer and the painting will not be in any kind of intellectual synchrony.[2]

Abstract art has been treated as a kind of artistic reductionism intended to lead to purity and the creation of an *atmospheric element,* which Kandinsky called the spiritual *Stimmung* ("atmosphere") of the work of art, or the *transcendent tendency.*

> Deliberate silence, deliberate negation, is a major way of sustaining the elusive spiritual atmosphere of the abstract work by ruthlessly reducing the artistic ("tasteful outer beauty") to an absolute minimum. Indeed silence attempts to eliminate beauty altogether. Paradoxically the absolutely silent becomes the radically beautiful, just as for Hegel absolutely abstract spirit becomes radically concrete being. The silence evokes an ecstatic sense of immediacy, an experience of radical beauty, breaking all the habits of mediation conventionally associated with perception. The achievement of silence is the logical conclusion of the process of negation that abstraction is. Conclusive silence is the irreducible outcome of reductive abstraction. (Kuspit, 1986, p. 314)

This position leads inevitably to the adoption of the essentialist view of silence (cf. §§2.2 and 2.3). Kuspit (1986, p. 314) recalls Poggioli's (1971) view that silence is pure and, therefore, enables art to free itself from "the prison of things." A few lines later, Kuspit (1986) adds:

> Poggioli remarked that Amèdèe Ozenfant was correct in thinking that silence represents "the need for extreme liberty and extreme intensity of feeling": absolute spiritual freedom. *The problem is how to create essential silence in abstract art today.* (p. 314; emphasis added)

Silence is conceptualized here as totally distinct from sound and as a discrete entity. I have rejected such an approach to conceptualizing silence, following Janicki (1990) who, after Popper (1972, 1976), has criticized the essentialist approach to the study of any phenomenon and to the study of language in particular. Janicki argues that linguistic work that pursues as its only goal correct and precise definitions of terms is futile. So is the search for absolute silence in art. Consider the following possible steps of reductionism in abstract art, leading to the achievement of the purest forms of silence. In his search for silence and spirituality, Kandinsky shifted away from figurative to abstract art. However, abstract art that employed gesture was discovered to have less silence than geometrical abstract art. Then, reducing the geometry of abstract painting to the shape of the canvas itself and covering it with monochromatic paint was considered even more silent. Finally, there are works that seem almost without any materiality (Kuspit, 1986, p. 315). We can also mention the creation of totally immaterial objects of art by Yves Klein. These were conceived of as immaterial paintings, "Immaterial Zones of Pictorial Sensibility," and air vibrations left for days in a place in a gallery where the artist had once given a speech (McEvilley, 1982).[3]

New criteria for defining the *absolute* can be established, new frames of analysis can be applied to the study of existing silent works (e.g., monochromatic paintings can be very rich in texture, the reflections on paintings can be treated as their integral part) and some abstract painters may altogether refuse to be called "abstract" (e.g., Mark Rothko).[4] Because of the possibility of relativizing all artistic experience and interpretation, the essentialist thinking in art can only lead to a dead end.

It is rather unfortunate then that art criticism confuses the most prototypical examples of silent art with the ultimate or the essential in silent abstract art. Of course, different artists and art critics will see different formal solutions as the most prototypical ones or, as they would be most likely to say, the ultimate and final instances of silence in art. Consider the following two examples:

> The ultimate in monotone, monochrome painting is the black or white canvas. As the two extremes, the so-called no-colors, white and black are associated with pure and impure, open and closed. The white painting is a "blank" canvas, where all is potential; the black painting has obviously been painted, but painted out, hidden, destroyed. (Lippard, 1981, p. 58)

> Three years after the Bolshevik success, the Russian Constructivist Alexander Rodchenko painted a monochrome canvas called *Pure Red*. There was a second, *Pure Yellow*, and a third, *Pure Blue*. The artist offered these primaries as pictorial essences—uninflected, unalloyed and final. (Ratcliff, 1981, p. 111)

For Lippard, the ultimate in monochrome painting is reached when a canvas has been painted all white or black. For Ratcliff (or Rodchenko), however, the same effect is achieved with the "uninflected, unalloyed and final" monochromes in the three primary colors: red, yellow, and blue.

In sum, I would like to reject once again the view that any final definition of *absolute silence* is possible: in art, communication, or any other field.

Instead of considering further theoretical disputes about the essence of silence and the ultimate in visual arts, I will now proceed to a discussion of the forms and functions silence has assumed in the monochrome painting of two artists: Yves Klein, and Robert Rauschenberg. Again, I am not defining silence in any particular, rigid way, but rather I identify a range of artistic forms and/or ideas that can be related to a generally functioning prototype of silence.

5.3.5.1 Yves Klein

Yves Klein's monochromes (mostly blue) were called by Restany "asthenic silence" and "pure contemplation" (McEvilley, 1982, p. 43). Restany (1982, p. 14) also saw Klein's reduction of forms as an attempt to increase the directness of communication. One can, of course, ask: What did Klein intend to communicate so directly? The answer is simple, although not trivial: His desire to transcend the limits of his material existence, to become a spiritual (and probably physical) unity with Space, to elevate the Void to the status of art form, to be able to fly. Blue was the dominant color of most of his material works because it was the color of the sky. The blue monochrome panels produced mainly between 1960 and 1961 are, according to Rosenthal (1982) "some of Klein's most sensuous and visually compelling works" (p. 101). Klein's monochromes could not be limitless in size to represent the vastness of space and the void. They "measure approximately 2 meters by 1½ meters" (Rosenthal, 1982, p. 101). The intended effect had to be achieved differently—not by increasing the size of the paintings but by turning inward into the paintings themselves. Consider one critic's approach to the interpretation of Klein's monochromes, which is very reminiscent of Tannen's frame analysis approach to the study of communication:

> Like much of Klein's work, these paintings call attention to surface. That is they concern the place where illusion and reality, or the deep space of painting and the real world, quite literally coalesce. They appear to the viewer to have deep space for several reasons. We

bring to paintings, even to paintings as flat and apparently imageless as these, our previous experience that paintings *are* windows into an ideal world. (Rosenthal, 1982, p. 101)

5.3.5.2 Robert Rauschenberg

In the early 1950s, Robert Rauschenberg painted a series of all-white, and later all-black paintings. In part, their effect was based on paradox and somewhat extreme formal properties. By using the two colors with minimal chromatic qualities, Rauschenberg tried, among other things, to reinstate into painting all colors on an equal basis.

> Their [paintings'] "emptiness" was simply the outcome of using color in stasis. Nothing is set in motion inside the picture, so nothing moves at the expense of anything else. (Forge, 1979, p. 12)

In a way this is reminiscent of the use of sound and silence, movement and stillness, and other opposites in Japanese art when one is necessary to define the other.

It is also interesting to note that on a perceptual level Rauschenberg's white and black paintings were not meant as any absolute expression of form. In an article written on the occasion of the artist's retrospective exhibition in 1977, a critic observed that both monochromatic paintings shown at the exhibition (one white and one black, both freshly repainted for the retrospective) "gently interact with their surroundings" (Stuckey, 1977, p. 79). The final effect of how the painting is perceived depends on, and is integral with, the external conditions:

> The white one adjusts most dramatically when an approaching spectator's shadow "appears" on the surface where he has taken light away from the picture. Rauschenberg is clearly a master of making images with only light. The shadows clearly are not part of the painting, but they are part of the spectator's encounter with it. They exist in the famous gap between art and life that Rauschenberg early promised to explore. . . . In the black paintings, too, are reflections of the spectator—very dim and dark ones, like the shadows of reflections. Again they belong to the viewer's optical nerves, not to the picture. (Stuckey, 1977, p. 79)

The monochromatic paintings are also subject to various framing and reframing processes. The above quote suggests an interpretation that requires framing of the painting together with the viewer and the light conditions of the room where it is hanging. It can be suggested then, that the whole gallery constitutes a frame for the monochromatic works.[5] However, as Forge suggests, more narrow reframings are also possible:

> If we say "a white canvas," we think of a bare canvas ready to be painted—an object. If we say "a white painting," we think of a painting in which white is the predominant color, either in the area or activity, an art work, in a different category from an object. What Rauschenberg's all-white paintings did was to allow him to see the self-colors of an object as pictorial color; and to claim for his pictorial color choice the unnegotiable integrity which is the attribute of objects. (Forge, 1979, p. 13)

The surface of the white paintings is very smooth, but in the black paintings the coat of paint was unevenly applied on a collagelike surface of a canvas covered with newspaper pages. Thus the black paintings give different visual effects discernible at the lower level framing processes. This is the level at which paint density, as well as the texture and the surface of the painting become the focus of the viewer's attention.

5.4 Formal Analogy Between Linguistic Silence and Its Visual Extensions

Several 20th-century artists have painted monochrome paintings; mostly white or black, but also in other colors. All these works have in their background a heterogeneity of artistic and philosophical thought (e.g., Hafif, 1981; Lippard, 1981; Ratcliff, 1981). Depending on a given painter, monotone painting has been connected with symbolism, mysticism, so-called new realism, formalism, reductionism and other interpretive trends.

Many a time, the work of monochrome painters has generated great controversies over the meaning and significance of such artistic gestures. For example, in a dispute over a series of white paintings by Robert Ryman, two critics—Kuspit (1979) and Hafif (1979)—attribute extremely opposite values to the silence of Ryman's paintings. Kuspit sees them as a negative, self-contained, undifferentiated set of objects detached from any reality and even from the referents of their titles (e.g., *State, Summit, Pilot, Region*). In his view, the paintings do not transcend anything and do not communicate anything sublime. They are entropy.[6] In her response to Kuspit, Hafif presents a totally opposite view of Ryman's white paintings. For her, the paintings in the series are different from each other, they carry nonliterary meaning, which is appropriately emphasized by the paintings' titles. Hafif admits that the reception of the paintings requires from the spectator more involvement and effort in interpretation than, for example, in contemplating a portrait. "Ryman's painting has a great deal to say to the viewer willing to engage it" (Hafif, 1979, p. 89). The author maintains further that the paintings in question are not detached from reality, but contemplative and human. Their formal simplicity is not a result of reductionism, but a tool of clarity and precision.

I have quoted the controversy above to indicate that a number of arguments about the meaning and reception of art remains in the realm of speculation and personal taste left out of any general theoretical framework, such as, for example, frame analysis (see also note 2). To a great extent, the arguments used by Hafif, Kuspit, and other art critics remain unfalsifiable statements. I believe, however, that both critics' positions outlined in the preceding paragraph, and a brief look at some painters' silent works, are useful to see that in its extensions into the visual, silence still retains the characteristics observed in its linguistic form. These features are the following:

Conventionality. Although we can talk about the most prototypical instances of silence (but not of its most prototypical meaning, see below), there is no "absolute" silence. Acoustic silence has to be defined in relation to sound (e.g., words), the presence or absence of which depends on the sensitivity of the receptive instrument (e.g., ear), one's expectations to hear something, or one's knowledge of what is not being said. In silent painting, artists and their critics have claimed the achievement of the absolute or ultimate form of expression. However, comparison of the works by various artists indicates great multiplicity of forms. The shape of the canvas, the type of materials, the method of applying the paint on the surface, texture, density, surface patterns, and so on are subject to variation and rule out the achievement of any "ultimately pure" form of expression.

Ambiguity. A given instance of silence or its extension lends itself to various interpretations; there is no one best or most prototypical meaning of silence (as is probably the case with words—verbal signs). If one, regardless of the context, remains silent, there is hardly any prototypical meaning attachable to this instance of silence. But if one says *dog* or *walk* in isolation, some prototypical concepts of "dog" and "walk" will probably be evoked in the minds of the speaker and hearer(s). A silent painting is by definition subject to many interpretations.

Bipolar Valency. Functionally, silence and its extensions fall on a continuum between a positive extreme and its negative counterpart (cf. §3.2). A silent painting may be an expression of a contemplative mind and may invite the spectator to contemplation or it may express a complete lack of any ideas, detach itself from any reality except its own, and communicate nothing (Dada).

Cool Medium. Silence is a cool medium of communication. It requires a high degree of participation and great involvement of the audience. Other things being equal, a listener has to invest more processing effort in maximizing the *relevance* of silence than of speech. The understanding and interpretation of a silent painting requires more filling in, background information, and/or involvement on the part of the spectator than in the interpretation of a landscape, still-life, or a portrait.

5.5 Other Art Forms

One can also find analogies between silence in painting and in other art forms. In her article about silent art, Lippard (1981) compares the monotone paintings with Stéphane Mallarmé's formally similar gesture in poetry

> when he proposed to reject symbolic interpretation of poetry and to leave nothing but the white page, which would be "evocative of all because it contained nothing." (p. 61)

Other poets have entertained similar ideas. For example, the Polish poet Anna Kamienska valued silence in her own poetry and wrote about it as a means of communication that is universal and more efficient than words. On another level, Kamienska's faith in the power of communicating with others in silence prompted her to include symbolically in one of her poetry collections a few blank pages (a project her publisher never agreed to). In this way, she wanted to manifest her dissatisfaction with the corruption and deterioration of language (words) closely connected with her experience of genocide during World War II and the triumph of a totalitarian system in postwar Poland (Szaruga, 1986).

When words fail poets, when artists find language inadequate to express themselves, they find refuge in silence. This rather linguistically naive conviction of the impurity and contamination of contemporary language is prevalent in much of recent art and art criticism. The solution for the artist trying to get free from the limitations of language is to move on to silence as the most adequate and "chaste" form of artistic expression (Sontag, 1966). Such, for example, is the idea of William Burroughs, for whom language (the Word), together with police and junk, are metaphors for *total control*. One of the ways of making people free is, for Burroughs, to silence their language (Hassan, 1971, pp. 249-250).

This is one level of the interrelationship of art and silence. To use a linguistic metaphor, this is the level of *form*, but there is also a level of *content*, where silence itself and the experience of silence become the subjects of artists' works.

The intermediate stage between the form and content levels of silence in art is the one in which silence is both the subject and form of expression in a work of art; 4′33″ of silence is probably the most famous example of a work of art that fits into this category. In this musical piece for piano by Cage, music is *not* played. Instead the attention of the listeners is shifted to the random acoustic signals reaching them during the 4′ 33″ of the performed composition. Here Cage uses silence as the main fabric of his piece—the performer and the instrument remain silent—but at the same time the piece is the composer's statement on the nonabsoluteness of silence. Cage suggests to his audience that absolute silence is fiction and that there are always some noises ("sounds not intended") that can be elevated to the status of music. The immediate inspiration for Cage to write 4′ 33″ was his own discovery that absolute silence did not exist, and the encouragement came from looking at Rauschenberg's blank canvases.

> This was brought home to him with great force when he was taken into a sound-proof room, called an anechoic chamber, in the physics laboratory at Harvard; instead of the total silence he had expected, he heard two sounds in the chamber, one high and one low, and was told when he came out that the high sound was his nervous system in operation and the low one was his blood circulating. (Tomkins, 1968, p. 118; see also Cage, 1961, p. 7)

An example of a literary piece in which silence is both its form and the subject matter is *A "concrete" poem* by Eugen Gomringer (1971). This poem consists of five lines with three words "silence" in each of them. In line three, the middle word "silence" is missing though there is a space left for it.

A "concrete" poem is iconic with respect to its topic in two ways. The most obvious and the most important one is the blank in the middle of line 3. It should correspond to an extended pause when the poem is said out loud. The other is the repetitive nature of the poem. As has been argued, undifferentiated repetition functionally approaches silence. Finally, silence (the signified) takes the shape of and exists in the only word used in the poem: *silence* (the signifier). *A "concrete" poem*, which seems like a simple poem, almost a literary joke, illustrates the complex nature of the concept of silence as a linguistic sign.

Quite a few studies of silence in literature exist. Roughly, they can be divided into two categories. One group is that of *functional-ethnographic analyses* of silences built into the body of literary works. The other is closer to literary studies proper and uses silence as an analytical tool in the study of literature. In chapter 1, I mentioned some works falling into the former category. Work belonging to the second category very often seems to be vague and unnecessarily complicated (see, e.g., Collier, 1984).

Hassan's (1967, 1971) treatment of silence in literature (or literary criticism) is close to my concept of extensions of silence (however, I do not always agree with Hassan's ideas). He takes silence to be a metaphor, a common denominator for a certain literary tradition: the avant-garde or antiliterature. For Hassan, who extends his metaphor of silence to the work of such authors as Sade, Hemingway, Kafka, Genet, Beckett, and Miller, silence operates on at least three levels: (1) The extreme psychological states such as madness, ecstasy, outrage, and so on are filled by silence when words have failed to provide adequate expression for them. (2) Silence conveys uncorrupted meaning (unlike corrupted words); the use of language in Romanticism was the most primitive and magical and it produced the first literature of silence. (3) Avant-garde literature challenges traditional literature in that the outcome of the former (i.e., silence) questions the main concern of the latter (i.e., the excellence of discourse).

The discussion of the uses of silence in literature and music in this section has not exhausted this vast topic (see, for example the references in note 12, chapter 1, and in McDonnell, 1982). I merely wanted to point out here the richness of the topic and to supplement the more elaborate treatment of silence in the visual arts.

5.6 Conclusion

In this chapter I looked at certain phenomena outside traditional linguistic studies of communication. The notion of communication has been extended beyond linguistics, and so has the concept of silence itself. It has been shown that nonlinguistic systems of communication, such as painting, can be studied with the same theoretical tools as linguistic communication. For example, the conceptualization of linguistic and nonlinguistic silences is equally possible via the ontological metaphors proposed by Lakoff and Johnson (1980; §3.5.1). In Hopper's painting the depicted scenes are structured through or framed in silence. Silence is a state in which the action of the paintings takes place. In the abstract monochromes silence is extended into the visual medium and treated as a direct form of expression by the artist. It is his or her form of artistic *activity* similar to the interpersonal silence in the dialogue between two people.

Linguistic and nonlinguistic silences have been shown to behave similarly within the theoretical frameworks of relevance theory and frame analysis. Linguistic silences and their visual extensions are both fairly weak forms of ostensive communication (§3.5.2), and their interpretation requires more processing effort—filling in—than speech and narrative, nonsilent paintings. Framing has turned out to be a powerful interpretive mechanism for identifying and analyzing different layers of nonlinguistic silences.

It is my contention that by showing the possibility of applying related or even identical types of methodologies and theories for the study of seemingly diverse social phenomena, we can find more consistency in the overwhelming diversity of human activities. By this I am not at all claiming that people in different cultures, professions, or intellectual orientations are identical or should behave in the same way. On the contrary, they are and should continue to be different from each other, which is necessary for self- and group identification, as well as for a pluralistic development of human thought. Nevertheless, it seems useful to be able to find common analytic denominators and to show consistent patterns of behavior in the seeming chaos of diversity.

Notes

1. Paintings need not only be viewed in regard to their communicative value or function. As a matter of fact, certain paintings or whole artistic schools and traditions can obviously be discussed solely in aesthetic terms, or as visual stimuli with a certain effect on the central nervous system and the senses of the viewers.

In the following discussion, paintings are going to be treated as painters' messages addressed to potential viewers.

2. The term *synchrony* has been borrowed from Hall (1983).

3. The following is an account of how immaterial paintings were created:

> In August 1959, while vacationing in Greece, Iris Clert [gallery owner] received a note from her assistant in Paris: "M. Klein came to take all his works. He told me that if a customer wished to buy one, I should say that his paintings are invisible, because immaterial, in the space of the gallery, and that if he wanted to buy one, it would suffice to write me a check. He was clear that the check should be quite visible. I think that M. Klein has gone mad." (quoted in McEvilley, 1982, p. 56)

4. Rothko, the "Old Master of New York abstraction" did not want to be called an abstract painter and maintained that his paintings were not mere abstractions and that they had a subject (Graham-Dixon, 1987). Moreover, Rothko claimed that his figures—mostly rectangles of pure, washed color with undefined edges—were as meaningful as the earlier figures he used to paint. He treated his paintings as statements on basic human emotions such as tragedy, ecstasy, and doom (Clearwater, 1987). The reactions to his painting were mixed: "Some found Rothko's luminous veils of color fraudulent voids, whose nothingness defied any reasonable expectation of what one should look at in a framed and painted rectangle of canvas, whereas others found them mysteriously silent and radiantly beautiful" (Rosenblum, 1987, p. 21).

5. Compare here other framing and reframing artistic experiments that also relate to the idea of extensions of silence. In April 1958, Yves Klein organized a show called "The Void." Framed by the gallery itself, there was nothing inside but bare, white walls that the artist presented to thousands of spectators. Camus's comment in the guest book read, "With the void, full powers" (McEvilley, 1982, pp. 49-50). There was nothing in the gallery to be seen by the spectators, but it was not empty. Two decades later, Roger Brown painted *Museum Without Paintings/A Commemorative of the Re-Opening of the Museum of Contemporary Art 1979.* In this case, the gallery is not full of immaterial pictures, as during the Klein show, but it is actually empty. The gallery does not frame the void and the intended silence of the artist but the silence of the gallery before another exhibition is installed in it is framed in the picture.

6. This is not to say that Kuspit views negatively all monotone painting; see, for example, his essay on the spiritual aspects of contemporary abstract art (Kuspit, 1986).

CHAPTER SIX

Conclusion

I used to know a medical student who revised material for all her exams with a fellow student and friend. They were both very diligent and involved in the program of their studies. Once my friend told me that when they were working on a particular section of medical science (for example, nephrology, cardiology, or orthopedics), they would both discover the developing symptoms of various diseases attacking their kidneys, hearts, or joints, respectively. Of course, the symptoms were gone once they had passed the exam in the given field. Some time later, I realized that linguists go through different but related experiences.

When linguists set their minds on certain problems, after a time they begin to notice examples supporting their theories everywhere. The pragmatic or (socio)linguistic patterns and paradigms they formulate seem to fit their surrounding reality perfectly well. Useful data seem to flow in constantly from the speech of friends, relatives, family members, casual acquaintances, and strangers. Linguists go around with their notebooks or tape recorders and perceive communication as if it were revolving around postvocalic *r*'s, reflexive pronouns, compliments, requests or apologies, sentences with *wh* movement transformations, puns, systems and parasystems, accommodation strategies, prosodic contours, paralinguistic systems, and so on.

Of course, when I began to work on silence I was also affected by a similar "disease." The more I thought about different forms and functions of silence the more support there was around me for the role of silence in communication. I was seeing it in my everyday encounters with others and in my perceptions of the ways people communicate and interact with each other.

It is my great hope that some of this silent disease has affected the readers of this book and that the disease is going to spread. If this book has the capacity of convincing its readers that silence is more important and widespread in communication than may be commonly admitted, then its primary aim has been fulfilled.

I have been open here to numerous frameworks for analyzing silence and by adopting them I have been able to suggest some unifying concepts and underlying theories that seem to warrant the formulation of hypotheses about what silence means and communicates. This overall eclectic approach should allow specialists from different fields of communication studies to find material relevant for their own work. I also believe that the interdisciplinary nature of this book will contribute to a better understanding of language and language study in different situations and in relation to nonlinguistic phenomena.

Silence has been presented here as a very diverse phenomenon. I have quoted and emphasized differences in the use of silence with respect to gender, culture, and situation, for example. I have spoken of the great ambiguity of silence, and the multitude of its forms ranging from the absence of audible noise to not saying what is expected in a given situation. I have identified as *silence* phenomena from several levels of linguistic analysis: psycholinguistics, phonetics, conversational analysis, pragmatics, and sociology of language as well as from the extralinguistic reality, for example, politics and the arts. Yet, I have also tried to find common denominators for all my considerations. I have sought underlying frameworks and theories to systematize the apparent chaos.

The underlying idea in this book has been to solve problems or provide tools for doing so. The problems that we have been mostly concerned with were predominantly theoretical: finding adequate frameworks of analysis for studying silence in various contexts. Thus I have suggested a three-way, prototype-oriented (Rosch, 1973, 1978) taxonomy of silences, largely based on the theory of metaphors (Lakoff & Johnson, 1980). I have suggested that silences be divided into states, activities, and formulaic (lexicalized) silences. The functioning of formulaic silence has been related to formulaic speech in highly ambiguous, face-threatening situations (Brown & Levinson, 1978/1987; Laver, 1981; Leach, 1976, 1977).

Silence as a state has been argued to structure communication (Philips, 1985) when the nonverbal and/or visual aspect of interaction gains more importance in interpreting what is going on in a given situation. Silences as activities have been understood as a type of nonverbal, conversational signals, which comprise propositional silences (Saville-Troike, 1985, in press), instances of *przemilczenie* ("failing to mention something") as well as psycholinguistic pauses. However, as far as the theory of relevance (Sperber & Wilson, 1986) can well account for the former two as types of ostensive communicative behavior, psycholinguistic pauses stand out and manifest cognitive meanings (not ostensive-inferential), which sets them apart from the other types of silence as activities.

Another theoretical aim of this book has been to argue for the nonessentialist approach (Janicki, 1990) to the study of silence, just as any other linguistic phenomenon. Relying on the theory of prototypes, I have argued for an indiscrete treatment of the category of silence. I have shown it as a range of linguistic items with talk at one end and silence at the other end of the continuum, with many intermediate, overlapping forms rather than two distinct, clear-cut and opposite categories.

When I made connections between the multifaceted notion of silence in conversation and its realization in the macro contexts of the media and politics, I called on relevance theory to explain why certain forms of talk in the media can have the effect of silence understood as lack of any communication, and the oppressive silence of dominated groups have been shown to follow the mechanisms of Leach's theory of taboo. Finally, I have turned to the visual extensions of acoustic silences in painting and, again, used the major theories presented in the earlier chapters, adding frame analysis as a useful paradigm that allows discovering and interpreting multiple layers of silence at different levels of abstraction.

I have also tried to bridge in this book two approaches that are usually treated as mutually exclusive: the relativist and the universalist. By stressing the obvious and important differences in the communication of different groups of people I have shown their uniqueness and, sometimes, perhaps, manifestations of different worldviews. At the same time, I have tried to point out that there are general underlying principles governing the occurrence and use of surface phenomena. On different levels, each approach is reasonably acceptable without denying the other.

One of the persistent themes of this book has been that silence means and communicates. The other has been that to make sense of this meaning we have to put our considerations into one or more coherent frameworks of analysis. It is hoped that the reader has been convinced of both these tenets. There is a lot more to be done, however. On the one hand, it is necessary to carry out further detailed case studies of the way silence works and/or is used in everyday conversations, literary genres, and political discourse and as a means of artistic expression. Its communicative, deceptive, and aesthetic qualities have to be assessed to raise our awareness about how communication works, how certain aspects of miscommunication are brought about, and how silence is used and can be enjoyed in creative ventures of artists. Maybe future studies will redefine what has been called here *silence* in other terms. *Implicature, inference, nontalk,* and *negative space* are some likely candidates suggested and used by other authors. No matter what label is used to refer to the phenomena covered in this book, we will still need theories to account and make sense out of them. Perhaps this book has pointed out some existing frameworks that are likely candidates for explaining the problems signaled here.

Several points taken for granted in the preceding pages welcome further empirical corroboration. The positivistic tenor of this book, emphasizing the significant role of silence in communication, may have been pointless in view of the actual attitudes of communicators from different cultures. Maybe it is not necessary to convince anyone that silence is a form communication. Attitudinal studies will be of great value here, as the first undertakings in this direction (Giles et al., 1991) have shown great diversity in the valuation of silence across (sub)cultures.

Another interesting question is how children are socialized into the use of silence (Saville-Troike, in press) and how they liberate themselves from it when they grow up.

Political discourse is an engaging topic in itself. However, adopting the view that more is concealed than revealed in politics, one can

look at the politicians' and media communicators' language through the prism of silence, and it can be very revealing about the possible and actual manipulative endeavors of the ruling elite. On the micro level, similar silent manipulation goes on in face-to-face interaction, and further studies should be able . . . .
. . . .

References

ABC News. (1987, November 13). Ethiopian drought bringing new famine (transcript). "Nightline."

ABC News. (1988a, February 22). Jimmy Swaggart confesses (transcript). "Nightline."

ABC News. (1988b, March 1). Trying to hide bad news (transcript). "Nightline."

ABC News. (1988c, March 11). Should American Jews criticize Israel? (transcript). "Nightline."

Activating the activists. (1988, April 25). *Newsweek*, p. 38

Albert, E. (1964). "Rhetoric," "logic," and "poetics" in Burundi: Cultural patterning of speech behavior. *American Anthropologist, 66*(6), Part 2, 35-54.

Allen, C. (1978). Failure of words, uses of silence: Djuna Barnes, Adrienne Rich, and Margaret Atwood. *Regionalism and Female Imagination, 4*(1), 1-7.

Amundsen, K. (1981). *The silenced majority: Women and American democracy*. Englewood Cliffs, NJ: Prentice-Hall.

Ardener. E. 1975. The problem of women revisited. In S. Ardener (Ed.), *Perceiving women* (pp. 19-27). London: J. M. Dent & Sons.

Bach, K., & Harnish, R. M. (1979). *Linguistic communication and speech acts*. Cambridge, MA: MIT Press.

Baer, R. A., Jr. (1976). Quaker silence, Catholic liturgy, and Pentecostal glossolalia—Some functional similarities. In R. P. Spittler (Ed.), *Perspectives on new Pentecostalism* (pp. 150-64). Grand Rapids, MI: Baker Book House.

Baker, S. J. (1955). The theory of silences. *Journal of General Psychology, 53*, 145-167.

Barbara, D. A. (1958). Don't be afraid of silence. *Today's Speech, VI*, 13-15.

Baron, D. (1986). *Grammar and gender*. New Heaven, CT: Yale University Press.

Barthes, R. (1967). *Writing degree zero* (A. Lavers & C. Smith, Trans.). New York: Hill & Wang. (Original work published 1953)

Barthes, R. (1986). *The rustle of language* (R. Howard, Trans.). New York: Hill & Wang. (Original work published 1984)

Basso, K. H. (1972). "To give up on words": Silence in Western Apache culture. In P. P. Giglioli (Ed.), *Language and social context* (pp. 67-86). Harmondsworth, UK: Penguin.

Basso, K. H. (1979). *Portraits of "the whiteman": linguistic play and cultural symbols among the Western Apache*. Cambridge, UK: Cambridge University Press.

Bateson, G. (1972). *Steps to an ecology of mind.* New York: Ballantine.

Bauman, R. (1974). Speaking in the light: The role of the Quaker minister. In R. Bauman & J. Sherzer (Eds.), *Explorations in the ethnography of speaking* (pp. 144-160). Cambridge, UK: Cambridge University Press.

Bauman, R. (1981). *Christ respects no man's person: The plain language of the early Quakers and the rhetoric of politeness* (Sociolinguistic Working Paper No. 88). Austin, TX: Southwest Educational Development Laboratory.

Bauman, R. (1983). *Let your words be few: Symbolism of speaking and silence among seventeenth-century Quakers.* Cambridge, UK: Cambridge University Press.

Beattie, G. & Bradbury, R. J. (1979). An experimental investigation of the modifiability of the temporal structure of spontaneous speech. *Journal of Psycholinguistic Research, 8*(3), 225-248.

Belsey, C. (1985). *The subject of tragedy: Identity and difference in renaissance drama.* London: Methuen.

Bennett, A. (1981). Interruptions and the interpretation of conversation. *Discourse Processes, 4,* 171-188.

Bindeman, S. L. (1981). *Heidegger and Wittgenstein: The poetics of silence.* Washington, DC: University Press of America

Binns, M. (1982). Music, theatre and silence. *Gambit: International Theatre Review, 10*(38), 5-16.

Birdwhistell, R. L. (1970). *Kinesics and context: Essays on body-motion communication.* Philadelphia: University of Pennsylvania Press.

The black book of Polish censorship. (1984). (J. Leftwich Curry, Ed. and Trans.). New York: Vintage Books.

Boardman, P. C. (1978). Beware the semantic trap: Language and propaganda. *ETC., 35.*

Bock, P. K. (1976). "I think but dare not speak": Silence in Elizabethan culture. *Journal of Anthropological Research, 32,* 285-294.

Bogart, L. (1984). *Strategy in advertising: Matching media and messages to markets and motivation* (2nd ed.). Chicago: Crain Books.

Bonikowska, M. P. (1988). The choice of opting out. *Applied Linguistics, 9*(2), 169-181.

Boomer, D. S. (1965). Hesitation and grammatical encoding. *Language and Speech, 8,* 148-158.

Bowers, J. W., Metts, S. M., & Duncanson, W. T. (1985). Emotion and interpersonal communication. In M. L. Knapp & G. R. Miller (Eds.), *Handbook of interpersonal communication* (pp. 500-550). Beverly Hills: Sage.

Bronner, S. J. (1982). "Your mother's like . . .": Formula in contemporary American ritual insults. *Maledicta, 6,* 199-210.

Brown, G., & Yule, G. (1983). *Discourse analysis.* Cambridge, UK: Cambridge University Press.

Brown, J. R. (1972). Harold Pinter: Words and silence. *The Birthday Party* and other plays. In J. R. Brown, *Theatre language: A study of Arden, Osborne, Pinter and Wesker* (pp. 15-54). New York: Taplinger.

Brown, P., & Levinson, S. (1987). *Politeness: Some universals in language usage.* Cambridge, UK: Cambridge University Press. (Original work published 1978)

Brownmiller, S. (1975). *Against our will: Men, women and rape.* New York: Bantam.

Brummet, B. (1980). Towards a theory of silence as a political strategy. *The Quarterly Journal of Speech, 66*, 289-303.

Burton, D. (1980). *Dialogue and discourse: A sociolinguistic approach to modern drama dialogue and naturally occurring conversation.* London: Routlege & Kegan Paul.

Bruneau, T. J. (1973). Communicative silences: Forms and functions. *The Journal of Communication, 23*, 17-46.

Bruneau, T. J. (1982). Communicative silences in cross-cultural perspective. *Media Development, 24*(4), 6-8.

Bruneau, T. J. (1985). Silencing and stilling processes: The creative and temporal bases of signs. *Semiotica, 56*, 279-290.

Cage, J. (1961). *Silence.* Middletown: Wesleyan University Press.

Cameron, D. (1985a). *Feminism & linguistic theory.* London: Macmillan.

Cameron, D. (1985b). What has gender got to do with sex? *Language and Communication, 5*(1), 19-27.

Capo, J. (1982). The shallow silence of the media world. *Media Development, 24*(4), 3-6.

Carston, R. (1984). Review of S. G. Pulman (1983). *Australian Journal of Linguistics, 4*(1), 89-99.

Caute, D. (1986). *The espionage of the saints: Two essays on silence and the state.* London: Hamish Hamilton.

CBS News. (1987, November 29). A few minutes with Andy Rooney (transcript). "60 Minutes."

Chafe, W. L. (1977). Creativity in verbalization and its implications for the nature of stored knowledge. In R. O. Freedle (Ed.), *Discourse production and comprehension* (pp. 41-55). Norwood, NJ: Ablex.

Chafe, W. L. (1985). Some reasons for hesitating. In D. Tannen & M. Saville-Troike (Eds.), *Perspectives on silence* (pp. 77-89). Norwood, NJ: Ablex.

Ciani, M. G. (Ed.). (1987). *The regions of silence: Studies on the difficulty of communicating.* Amsterdam: J. C. Gieben.

Clearwater, B. (1987). Selected statements by Mark Rothko. In *Mark Rothko 1903-1970* (pp. 66-75). London: Tate Gallery Publications.

Clifton, T. (1976). The poetics of musical silence. *The Musical Quarterly, 62*(2), 163-181.

Collier, P. (1984). Beyond words: Language and silence in Bataille's fiction. In P. Buck (Ed.), *Violent silence* (pp. 65-73). London: Georges Bataille Event.

Cook, J. J. (1964). Silence in psychotherapy. *Journal of Counseling Psychology, 11*(1), 42-46.

Crick, M. (1976). *Explorations in language and meaning.* London: Malaby Press.

Crown, C. L., & Feldstein, S. (1985). Psychological correlates of silence and sound in conversational interaction. In D. Tannen & M. Saville-Troike (Eds.), *Perspectives on silence* (pp. 31-54). Norwood, NJ: Ablex.

Cruttenden, A. (1986). *Intonation.* Cambridge, UK: Cambridge University Press.

Crystal, D. (1987). *The Cambridge encyclopedia of language.* Cambridge, UK: Cambridge University Press.

Cubberly, N. (1984-1985). Your mother has yaws: Verbal abuse at Ulithi. *Maledicta, 8*, 154-157.

Daly, M. (1973). *Beyond God the Father: Toward a philosophy of women's liberation.* Boston: Beacon Press.

Daly, M. (1978). *Gyn/Ecology: The methaetics of radical feminism.* Boston: Beacon Press.

Dambska, I. (1975). O funkcjach semiotycznych milczenia. *Znaki i mysli: wybór pism z semiotyki, teorii nauki i historii filozofii. Towarzystwo Naukow w Toruniu. Prace Wydzialu Filologiczno-Filozoficznego 25,* 93-105.

Dauenhauer, B. P. (1980). *Silence, the phenomenon and its ontological significance.* Bloomington: Indiana University Press.

Davidson, J. (1984). Subsequent versions of invitations, offers, requests, and proposals dealing with potential or actual rejection. In J. M. Atkinson & J. M. Heritage (Eds.), *Structures of social action: Studies in conversational analysis* (pp. 102-128). Cambridge, UK: Cambridge University Press.

Dressler, W. U. (1988). A linguistic classification of phonological paraphasias. In W. U. Dressler & J. Stark (Eds.), *Linguistic analysis of aphasic language* (pp. 1-22). New York: Springer.

Duez, D. (1982). Silent and non-silent pauses in three speech styles. *Language and Speech, 25,* 11-28.

Duez, D. (1985). Perception of silent pauses in continuous speech. *Language and Speech, 28,* 377-389.

Dumont, R. V., Jr. (1972). Learning English and how to be silent: Studies in Sioux and Cherokee classrooms. In C. B. Cazden, V. P. John, & D. Hymes (Eds.), *Functions of language in the classroom* (pp. 344-370). Prospect Heights, IL: Waveland Press.

Ellul, J. (1965). *Propaganda: The formation of men's attitudes* (K. Kellen & J. Lerner, Trans.). New York: Vintage Books.

Enninger, W. (1983). Silence(s) across cultures. *INTUS NEWS/-NUUS, 7*(1), 36-44.

Enninger, W. (1985). Significant silence among the Amish. In S. M. Benjamin & M. Ritterson (Eds.), *Papers from the third conference on German-Americana in the Eastern United States. November 6-7, 1982* (pp. 149-159). Radford, VA: Radford University, Intercultural Communications Center.

Enninger, W. (1987). What interactants do with non-talk across cultures. In K. Knapp, W. Enninger, & A. Knapp-Potthoff (Eds.), *Analyzing intercultural communication* (pp. 269-302). Berlin: Mouton de Gruyter.

Erickson, K. V., & Schmidt, W. V. (1982). Presidential political silence: Rhetoric and the Rose Garden strategy. *The Southern Speech Communication Journal, 47,* 402-421.

Farr, J. N. (1962). How to communicate with silence. *Nation's Business, 50*(6), 96-97.

Feldstein, S., & Welkowitz, J. (1987). A chronography of conversation: In defense of an objective approach. In A. Siegman & S. Feldstein (Eds.), *Nonverbal behavior and communication* (2nd ed., pp. 435-499). Hillsdale, NJ: Erlbaum.

Fibicher. (1982). The art of silence: Poetry and painting. *Media Development, 24*(4), 13-17.

Fillmore, C. J. (1984). Remarks on contrastive pragmatics. In J. Fisiak (Ed.), *Contrastive linguistics: prospects and problems* (pp. 119-141). Berlin: Mouton.

Foccardi, D. (1987). Religious silence and reticence in Pausanias. In M. G. Ciani (Ed.), *The regions of silence: Studies on the difficulty of communicating* (pp. 67-114). Amsterdam: J. C. Gieben.

Forge, A. (1979). *Rauschenberg*. New York: Abram.

Frazer, J. (1959). *The new golden bough* (T. H. Gaster, Ed.). New York: Mentor.

Ganguly, S. N. (1968-1969). Culture, communication and silence. *Philosophy and Phenomenological Research, 29*, 182-200.

Gardner, P. M. (1966). Symmetric respect and memorate knowledge: The structure and ecology of individualistic culture. *Southwestern Journal of Anthropology, 22*, 389-415.

Gardner, P. M. (1986). Review of D. Tannen and M. Saville-Troike. (1985). *American Anthropologist, 88*, 509-510.

Gazeta Wyborcza. (1989, August 10). Zgodne milczenie (Agreed silence). No. 67, p. 6.

Giles, H., Coupland, N., & Wiemann, J. M. (1991). "Talk is cheap" but "My word is my bond": Beliefs about talk. In K. Bolton & H. Kwok (Eds.), *Sociolinguistics today: Eastern and Western perspectives* (pp. 218-243). London: Routledge.

Gilmore, P. (1985). Silence and sulking: Emotional displays in the classroom. In D. Tannen & M. Saville-Troike (Eds.), *Perspectives on silence* (pp. 139-162). Norwood, NJ: Ablex.

Glassie, H. (1982). *Passing the time in Ballymenone: Culture and history of an Ulster community*. Philadelphia: University of Philadelphia Press.

Goffman, E. (1974). *Frame analysis: An essay on the organization of experience*. New York: Harper & Row.

Goldman-Eisler, F. (1967). Sequential temporal patterns and cognitive processes in speech. *Language and Speech, 9*, 207-216.

Goldsen, R. E. (1978). Why television advertising is deceptive and unfair. *ETC., 35*, 354-375.

Goldstein, D. E. (1987). Review of Tannen and Saville-Troike (1985). *Language in Society, 16*, 565-569.

Gomringer, E. (1971). *Poetry as system*. Glenview, IL: A. C. Winkler.

Graham-Dixon, A. (1987, June 17). Beyond the material [Review of the Tate Gallery's retrospective of Mark Rothko]. *The Independent*, p. 15.

Gray, B. (1969). *Style: The problem and its solution*. The Hague: Mouton.

Grice, H. P. (1975). Logic and conversation. In P. Cole & J. L. Morgan (Eds.), *Syntax and semantics. Vol. 3: Speech acts* (pp. 41-58). New York: Academic Press

Gunderson, R. G. (1961). Lincoln and the policy of eloquent silence: November, 1860, to March, 1861. *The Quarterly Journal of Speech, 47*, 1-9.

Hafif, M. (1979, September). Robert Ryman: Another view. *Art in America, 67*, 88-89.

Hafif, M. (1981, April). Getting on with painting. *Art in America, 69*, 132-139.

Hall, E. T. (1983). *The dance of life: The other dimension of time*. Garden City, NY: Doubleday.

Harris, Z. (1951). *Methods in structural linguistics*. Chicago: Chicago University Press.

Hart: The invisible man. (1988, February 22). *Newsweek*, p. 233.

Hartley, M. (1982). The communication challenge in Cisterian monastic life. *Media Development, 24*(4), 22-25.

Hassan, I. (1967). *The literature of silence: Henry Miller and Samuel Beckett*. New York: Knopf.

Hassan, I. (1971). *The dismemberment of Orpheus: Toward a postmodern literature*. New York: Oxford University Press.

Hill, A. O. (1986). *Mother tongue, father time: A decade of linguistic revolt*. Bloomington: Indiana University Press.

Hinde, R. A. (Ed.). (1972). *Non-verbal communication*. Cambridge, UK: Cambridge University Press.

Holmes, J., & Brown, D. F. (1987). Teachers and students learning about compliments. *TESOL Quarterly, 21*(3), 523-546.

Holowka, T. (1986). *Myslenie potoczne*. Warszawa: PIW

Houston, M., & Kramarae, C. (1991). Speaking from silence: Methods of silencing and of resistance. *Discourse & Society, 2*(4), 387-399.

Hudson, R. (1980). *Sociolinguistics*. Cambridge, UK: Cambridge University Press.

Hymes, D. (1962). The ethnography of speaking. In T. Galdwin & W. C. Sturevant (Eds.), *Anthropology and human behavior* (pp. 13-53). Washington, DC: Anthropological Society of Washington.

Hymes, D. (1974). *Foundations in sociolinguistics: An ethnographic approach*. Philadelphia: University of Pennsylvania Press.

Informative note. (1976, July 9). No. 55. In *The black book of Polish censorship* (J. Leftwich Curry, Ed. and Trans.; pp. 105-106). New York: Vintage Books.

Jackson, N. (1974). *Meeting silence: The religious uses of group silence*. Unpublished doctoral dissertation, Washington University, St. Louis.

Jaksa J. A., & Stech, E. L. (1978). Communication to enhance silence: The Trappist experience. *Journal of Communication, 28*, 14-18.

Janicki, K. (1987). On understanding misunderstanding: Some further support for prototype linguistics. *Folia Linguistica, 21*(2-4), 463-470.

Janicki, K. (1989). A rebuttal of essentialist sociolinguistics. *International Journal of the Sociology of Language, 78*, 93-105.

Janicki, K. (1990). *Toward non-essentialist sociolinguistics*. Berlin: Mouton de Gruyter.

Janicki, K., & Jaworski, A. (1990, September). *Toward non-Aristotelian sociolinguistics*. Paper presented at the 23rd Annual Societas Linguistica Europaea Meeting. Berne, Switzerland.

Jaworski, A. (1986). *A linguistic picture of women's position in society*. Frankfurt am Main: Peter Lang.

Jaworski, A. (1990). The acquisition and perception of formulaic language and foreign language teaching. *Multilingua, 9*(4), 379-411.

Jensen, V. (1973). Communicative functions of silence. *ETC., 30*, 249-257.

Johannesen, R. (1974). The functions of silence: A plea for communication research. *Western Speech, 38*, 25-35.

John, V. P. (1972). Styles of learning—styles of teaching: Reflections on the education of Navajo children. In C. B. Cazden, V. P. John, & D. Hymes (Eds.), *Functions of language in the classroom* (pp. 331-343). Prospect Heights, IL: Waveland Press.

Johnson, F. L., & Davis, L. K. (1979). Hesitation phenomena in televised family conversations in the U.S.A. *International Journal of Psycholinguistics, 6*(1), 29-45.

Kapuscinski, R. (1976). *Chrystus z karabinem na ramieniu*. Warszawa: Czytelnik.

Keenan, E. O. (1974). The universality of conversational implicatures. In R. W. Fasold & R. W. Shuy (Eds.), *Studies in language variation* (pp. 255-268). Washington, DC: Georgetown University Press.

Kelsey, M. T. (1976). *The other side of silence: A guide to Christian meditation.* New York: Paulist Press.

Kendon, A. (1985). Some uses of gesture. In D. Tannen & M. Saville-Troike (Eds.), *Perspectives on silence* (pp. 215-234). Norwood, NJ: Ablex.

Knapp, M. L. (1972). *Nonverbal communication in human interaction.* New York: Holt, Rinehart & Winston.

Koch, S. (1974). *Stargazer: Andy Warhol's world and his films.* London: Calder & Boyars.

Korzybski, A. (1933). *Science and sanity: An introduction to non-Aristotelian systems and general semantics.* Lakeville, CT: Institute of General Semantics.

Kowal, S., O'Connell, D. C., and Sabin, E. J. (1975). Development of temporal patterning and vocal hesitations in spontaneous narratives. *Journal of Psycholinguistic Research, 4*(3), 195-207.

Kramarae, C. (1981). *Women and men speaking.* Rowley, MA: Newbury House.

Kramarae, C. (1992). Punctuating the dictionary. *International Journal of the Sociology of Language, 94,* 135-154.

Kuspit, D. B. (1979, July-August). Ryman, Golub: Two painters, two positions. *Art in America, 67,* 88-90.

Kuspit, D. (1986). Concerning the spiritual in contemporary art. In Los Angeles County Museum of Art (Ed.), *The spiritual in contemporary art: abstract painting 1890-1985* (pp. 313-325). Los Angeles: Abevielle Press.

LaForge, P. G. (1983). *Counseling and culture in second language acquisition.* Oxford, UK: Pergamon Press.

Lakoff, R. (1973). The logic of politeness; or, minding your p's and q's. In *Papers from the ninth Regional Meeting of the Chicago Linguistic Society* (pp. 292-305). Chicago: Chicago Linguistic Society.

Lakoff, G., & Johnson, M. (1980). *Metaphors we live by.* Chicago: University of Chicago Press.

Lakoff, R. T., & Tannen, D. (1984). Communicative strategies and metastrategies in a pragmatic theory: The case of *Scenes from a marriage. Semiotica, 17*(3-4), 323-346.

Lavandera, B. R. (1986). Intertextual relationships: "Missing people" in Argentina. In D. Tannen & J. E. Alatis (Eds.), *Georgetown University Round Table on Language and Linguistics 1985* (pp. 121-139). Washington, DC: Georgetown University Press.

Laver, J. D. M. H. (1981). Linguistic routines and politeness in greeting and parting. In F. Coulmas (Ed.), *Conversational routine: Explorations in standardized communication situations and prepatterned speech* (pp. 289-304). The Hague: Mouton.

Leach, E. R. (1964). Anthropological aspects of language: Animal categories and verbal abuse. In E. H. Lenneberg (Ed.), *New directions in the study of language* (pp. 23-63). Cambridge, MA: MIT Press.

Leach, E. R. (1976). *Culture and communication: The logic by which symbols are connected. An introduction to the use of structuralist analysis in social anthropology.* Cambridge, UK: Cambridge University Press.

Leach, E. (1977). *Custom, law, and terrorist violence.* Edinburgh, UK: Edinburgh University Press.

Leach, E. (1982). *Social anthropology.* Oxford, UK: Oxford University Press.

Lebra, T. S. (1987). The cultural significance of silence in Japanese communication. *Multilingua,* (6-4), 343-357.

Leech, G. N. (1966). *English in advertising: A linguistic study of advertising in Britain.* London: Longman.

Lehtonen, J., & Sajavaara, K. (1985). The silent Finn. In D. Tannen & M. Saville-Troike (Eds.), *Perspectives on silence* (pp. 193-201). Norwood, NJ: Ablex.

Lehtonen, J., Sajavaara, K., & Manninen, S. (1985). Communication apprehension and attitudes toward a foreign language. *Working Papers on Bilingualism, 5,* 53-62.

Leski, K. (1990, October 16). Mazowiecki i Walesa czyli dwie kampanie [Mazowiecki and Walesa two campaigns] *Gazeta Wyborcza,* (241), p. 3.

Levinson, S. C. (1983). *Pragmatics.* Cambridge, UK: Cambridge University Press.

Lieberman, P. (1967). *Intonation, perception and language* (Research Monograph Vol. 38). Cambridge, MA: MIT Press.

Lippard, L. R. (1981, January-February). The silent art. *Art in America, 55,* 58-63.

Lynch, J. J. (1977). *The broken heart: The medical consequences of loneliness.* New York: Basic Books.

Maclay, H., & Osgood, C. E. (1959). Hesitation phenomenon in spontaneous English speech. *Word, 15,* 19-44.

Malinowski, B. (1972). Phatic communion. In J. Laver & S. Hutcheson (Eds.), *Communication in face to face interaction* (pp. 146-152). Harmondsworth, UK: Penguin. (Original work published 1923)

Maltz, D. N. (1985). Joyful noise and reverent silence: The significance of noise in Pentecostal worship. In D. Tannen & M. Saville-Troike (Eds.), *Perspectives on silence* (pp. 113-137). Norwood, NJ: Ablex.

Manes, J., & Wolfson, N. (1981). The compliment formula. In F. Coulmas (Ed.), *Conversational routine: Explorations in standardized communication situations and prepatterned speech* (pp. 115-131). The Hague: Mouton.

McDonnell, J. (1982). Bibliography on silence in communication. *Media Development, 24*(4), 38-40.

McEvilley, T. (1982). Yves Klein: Conquistador of the void. In *Yves Klein 1928-1962: A retrospective* (pp. 19-86). Houston: Rice University Institute of Art in association with The Art Publisher, Inc.

McGuire, P. C. (1985). *Speechless dialect: Shakespeare's open silences.* Berkeley: University of California Press.

McLuhan, M. (1964). *Understanding media: The extensions of man* (2nd ed.). New York: Mentor.

Meerloo, J. A. M. (1975). The strategy of silence. *Communication, 2,* 69-79.

Mendez, C. W. (1972). I need a little language. *Virginia Woolf Quarterly, 1*(1), 87-105.

Mendez, C. W. (1978). Creative breakthrough: Sequence and the blade of consciousness in Virginia Woolf's *The Waves.* In D. Butturff & E. L. Epstein (Eds.), *Women's language and style* (pp. 84-98A). Akron, OH: University of Akron Press.

Mendez, C. W. (1980). Virginia Woolf and the voices of silence. *Language and Style, 13*(4), 94-112.

Merton, T. (1982). Facing oneself in silence. *Media Development, 24*(4), 20-21. (Original work published 1979)

Milroy, L. (1980). *Language and social networks.* Oxford, UK: Basil Blackwell.

Milroy, L. (1987). *Observing and analyzing natural language: A critical account of sociolinguistic methodology.* Oxford, UK: Basil Blackwell.

Miyoshi, M. (1974). *Accomplices of silence: The modern Japanese novel.* Berkeley: University of California Press.

Mora, F. (1987). Religious silence in Herodotus and in the Athenian theatre. In M. G. Ciani (Ed.), *The regions of silence: Studies on the difficulty of communicating* (pp. 41-65). Amsterdam: J. C. Gieben.

Moran, T. P. (1979). Propaganda as pseudocommunication. *ETC., 36,* 181-197.

Morgan, J. L., & Green, G. M. (1987). On the search for relevance. *Behavioral and Brain Sciences, 10*(4), 726-727.

Muchinsky, D. (1985). The unnatural approach: Language learning in Poland (Report). Washington, DC: U.S. Department of Education, National Institute of Education and Educational Resources Information Center.

Murphy, M. (1970). Silence, the word, and Indian rhetoric. *College Composition and Communication, 21,* 359-363.

Murray, S. O. (1985). Toward a model of members' methods for recognizing interruptions. *Language in Society, 14,* 31-40.

Murray, S. O. (1987). Power and solidarity in "interruption": A critique of the Santa Barbara school conception and its application by Orcutt and Harvey (1985). *Symbolic Interaction, 10*(1), 101-110.

Murray, S. O., & Covelli, L. H. (1988). Women and men speaking at the same time. *Journal of Pragmatics, 12*(1), 103-111.

National Education Association. (1972). The invisible minority. In R. D. Abrahams & R. C. Troike (Eds.), *Language and cultural diversity in American education* (pp. 55-66). Englewood Cliffs, NJ: Prentice-Hall. (Original work published 1966)

Neher, A. (1981). *The exile of the word: From the silence of the Bible to the silence of Auschwitz* (D. Maisel, Trans.). Philadelphia: Jewish Publication Society of America.

Nwoye, G. (1985). Eloquent silence among the Igbo of Nigeria. In D. Tannen & M. Saville-Troike (Eds.), *Perspectives on silence* (pp. 185-191). Norwood, NJ: Ablex.

O'Barr, W. M. (1982). *Controlling the effects of presentational style. Linguistic evidence—Language, power, and strategy in the courtroom.* New York: Academic Press.

O'Doherty, B. (n.d.). Hopper's silence: A film memoir by Brian O'Doherty (VHS). The Philip Morris Collection (available in the U.S. Embassy Library, Warsaw).

Öhman, S. (1989). Problems and pseudo-problems in linguistics: Presentation of a research project. *Reports from Uppsala University Department of Linguistics,* (18), 29-41.

O'Kelly, T. (1982). Land of loud silences: Understanding Japanese communicative behaviour. *Media Development, 24*(4), 30-33.

Oleksy, W. (1984). Towards pragmatic contrastive analysis. In J. Fisiak (Ed.), *Contrastive linguistics: Prospects and problems* (pp. 349-364). Berlin: Mouton.

Olsen, T. (1978). *Silences.* New York: Delacorte Press/Seymour Lawrence.

O'Neil, N., & O'Neil, G. (1972). *Open marriage.* New York: Avon Books.

Opie, I., & Opie, P. (1959). *The lore and language of schoolchildren.* London: Grandma.

Pace Nilsen, A. (1986). Sexism in English: A feminist view. In P. Eschholz, A. Rosa, & V. Clark (Eds.), *Language awareness* (pp. 301-308). New York: St. Martin's Press.

Party justifies its "triumph"(1989b, June 6). *The Times,* p. 1.

Peking protesters massacred. (1989a, June 5). *The Times,* p. 2.

Penelope, J. S., & Wolfe, S. J. (1983). Consciousness as style; style as aesthetic. In B. Thorne, C. Kramarae, & N. Henley (Eds.), Language, gender, and society (pp. 125-139). Rowley, MA: Newbury House.

Petersen, W. (1960). Stone garden. In N. Wilson Rose (Ed.), *The world of Zen: An East-West anthology.* New York: Random House.

Philips, S. U. (1972). Participant structures and communicative competence: Warm Springs children in community and classroom. In C. B. Cazden, V. P. John, & D. Hymes (Eds.), *Functions of language in the classroom* (pp. 370-394). Prospect Heights, IL: Waveland Press.

Philips, S. U. (1976). Some sources of cultural variability in the regulation of talk. *Language in Society* 5:81-95.

Philips, S. U. (1983). *The invisible culture: Communication in classroom and community on the Warm Springs Indian reservation.* New York: Longman.

Philips, S. U. (1985). Interaction structured through talk and interaction structured through "silence." In D. Tannen & M. Saville-Troike (Eds.), *Perspectives on silence* (pp. 205-213). Norwood, NJ: Ablex.

Picard, M. (1948). *The world of silence* (S. Godman, Trans.). London: Harvill.

Pike, K. L. (1945). *The intonation of American English.* Ann Arbor: University of Michigan Press.

Pittenger, R. E., Hockett, C. F., & Danehy, J. J. (1960). *The first five minutes: A sample of microscopic interview analysis.* Ithaca, NY: Paul Martineau.

Poggioli, R. (1971). *The theory of the avant-garde.* New York: Harper & Row.

Popper, K. (1945). *The open society and its enemies* (Vol. 1 & 2). London: Routledge & Kegan Paul.

Popper, K. (1972). *Objective knowledge.* Oxford, UK: Oxford University Press.

Popper, K. (1976). *Unended quest.* London: Fontana/Collins.

Popper, K., & Eccles, J. C. (1983). *The self and its brain: An argument for interactionalism.* London: Routlege & Kegan Paul. (Original work published 1977)

Poyatos, F. (1981). Silence and stillness: Toward a new status of non-activity. *Kodikas/Kode, 3,* 3-26.

Poyatos, F. (1983). *New perspectives in nonverbal communication.* Oxford, UK: Pergamon Press.

Pulman, S. G. (1983). *Word meaning and belief.* Norwood, NJ: Ablex.

Ratcliff, C. (1981, April). Mostly monochrome. *Art in America, 69,* 111-131.

Reisman, K. (1974). Contrapuntal conversations in an Antiguan village. In R. Bauman & J. Sherzer (Eds.), *Explorations in the ethnography of speaking* (pp. 110-124). Cambridge, UK: Cambridge University Press.

Restany, P. (1982). Who is Yves Klein? In *Yves Klein 1928-1962: A retrospective* (pp. 13-17). Houston: Rice University Institute of Art in association with The Art Publisher, Inc.

Rice, G. P. (1961). The right to be silent. *Quarterly Journal of Speech, 47,* 349-354.

Rich, A. (1978, Summer). The transformation of silence into language and action (panel discussion). *Sinister Wisdom, 6,* 17-25.

Rich, A. (1984). *On lies, secrets and silence: Selected prose 1966-1978.* London: Virago. (Original work published 1979)

Richardson, E. P. (1956). *Painting in America: From 1502 to the present.* New York: Thomas Y. Crowell.

Rokoszowa, J. (1983). Jezyk a milczenie. *Biuletyn Polskiego Towarzystwa Jezykoznawczego, 40,* 129-137.

Rooney, A. A. (1987). A conspiracy against silence. In A. A. Rooney, *Word for Word* (pp. 172-174). New York: Berkley Books.

Rosch, E. (1973). Natural categories. *Cognitive Psychology, 4,* 328-350.

Rosch, E. (1978). Principles of categorization. In E. Rosch & B. L. Lloyd (Eds.), *Cognition and categorization* (pp. 27-48). Hillsdale, NJ: Erlbaum.

Rosch, E., & C. B. Mervis. (1975). Family resemblances: Studies in the internal structure of categorization. *Cognitive Psychology, 7,* 532-547.

Rose, B. (1977). *American painting: The twentieth century* (2nd ed.). London: Macmillan.

Rosenblum, R. (1987). Notes on Rothko and tradition. In *Mark Rothko 1903-1970* (pp. 21-31). London: Tate Gallery Publications.

Rosenthal, N. (1982). Assisted levitation: The art of Yves Klein. In *Yves Klein 1928-1962: A retrospective* (pp. 89-135). Houston: Rice University Institute of Art in association with The Art Publisher, Inc.

Rovine, H. (1987). *Silence in Shakespeare: Drama, power, and gender.* Ann Arbor: UMI Research Press.

Rowe, M. B. (1974). Pausing phenomena: Influence on the quality of instruction. *Journal of Psycholinguistic Research, 3*(3) 203-224.

Sacks, H., Schegloff, E., & Jefferson, G. (1974). A simplest systematics for organization of turn-taking in conversation. *Language, 50,* 696-735.

Samarin, W. J. (1965). Language of silence. *Practical Anthropology, 12*(3), 115-119.

Sansom, B. (1982). The sick who do not speak. In D. Parkin (Ed.), *Semantic anthropology* (pp. 183-195). London: Academic Press.

Sapir, E. (1937). Symbolism. In *Encyclopedia of social sciences* (Vol. 14, pp. 492-495). New York: Macmillan.

Sattel, J. W. (1983). Men, inexpressiveness, and power. In B. Thorne, C. Kramarae, & N. Henley (Eds.), *Language, gender, and society* (pp. 119-124). Rowley, MA: Newbury House.

Saunders, G. R. (1985). Silence and noise as emotion management styles: An Italian case. In D. Tannen & M. Saville-Troike (Eds.), *Perspectives on silence* (pp. 165-183). Norwood, NJ: Ablex.

Saville-Troike, M. (1982). *The ethnography of communication: An introduction.* Oxford, UK: Basil Blackwell.

Saville-Troike, M. (1985). The place of silence in an integrated theory of communication. In D. Tannen & M. Saville-Troike (Eds.), *Perspectives on silence* (pp. 3-18). Norwood, NJ: Ablex.

Saville-Troike, M. (1988). Private speech: Evidence for second language learning strategies during the "silent" period. *Journal of Child Language, 15*(3) 567-590.

Saville-Troike. (in press). Silence. In R. Asher (Ed.), *The international encyclopedia of language and linguistics.* Oxford, UK: Pergamon Press.

Schiffrin, D. (1987). *Discourse markers*. Cambridge: Cambridge University Press.

Schneider, K. R. (1987). Topics selection in phatic communion. *Multilingua*, (6-3), 247-256.

Scollon, R. (1981). *Tempo, density and silence: Rhythms in ordinary talk*. Fairbanks: University of Alaska, Center for Cross-Cultural Studies.

Scollon, R. (1982). The rhythmic integration of ordinary talk. In D. Tannen (Ed.), *Georgetown University Round Table on Language and Linguistics 1981* (pp. 335-349). Washington, DC: Georgetown University Press.

Scollon, R. (1985). The machine stops: Silence in the metaphor of malfunction. In D. Tannen & M. Saville-Troike (Eds.), *Perspectives on silence* (pp. 21-30). Norwood, NJ: Ablex.

Scollon, R., & Scollon, S. (1987). *Responsive communication*. Haines, AK: Black Current Press.

Scott, R. L. (1972). Rhetoric and silence. *Western Speech, 36*, 146-158.

Sennet, R., & Cobb, J. (1972). *The hidden injuries of class*. New York: Knopf.

Sherzer, J. (1977). The ethnography of speaking: A critical appraisal. In M. Saville-Troike (Ed.), *Linguistics and anthropology* (pp. 43-57). Washington, DC: Georgetown University Press.

Smith, H. A. (1984). State of the art of nonverbal behavior in teaching. In A. Wolfgang (Ed.), *Nonverbal behavior: Perspectives, applications, intercultural insights* (pp. 171-202). Lewiston, NY: C. J. Hografe.

Sontag, S. (1966). The aesthetics of silence. In *Styles of radical will* (pp. 3-34). New York: Farrar, Straus.

Sorrels, B. D. (1983). *The nonsexist communicator: Solving problems of gender and awkwardness in modern English*. Englewood Cliffs, NJ: Prentice-Hall.

Spender, D. (1980). *Man made language*. London: Routledge & Kegan Paul.

Spender, D. (1982). *Invisible women: The schooling scandal*. London: Writers & Readers.

Sperber, D., & Wilson, D. (1986). *Relevance: Communication and cognition*. Oxford, UK: Basil Blackwell.

Sperber, D., & Wilson, D. (1987). Response to Morgan and Green. *Behavioral and Brain Sciences, 10*(2), 746-747.

Stanley, J. P. (1977). Sexist grammar. *College English, 39*(7), 800-811.

Steggink, O. (1982). Silence and solitude are the path of love. *Media Development, 24*(4), 17-20.

Steiner, G. (1976). The retreat from the word. In *Language and silence: Essays on language*. New York: Atheneum.

Steiner, G. (1982). "O word, thou word that I lack!": Schoenberg's *Moses und Aron*. *Media Development, 24*(4), 9-12. (Original work published 1979)

Strelan, J. (1982). When the church should fall silent. *Media Development, 24*(4), 37.

Stuckey, C. F. (1977, March-April). Reading Rauschenberg. *Art in America, 65*, 74-84.

Suzuki, D. T. (1938). *Zen Buddhism and its influence on Japanese culture*. Kyoto: Eastern Buddhist Society.

Szaruga, L. (1986). Slowa ku milczeniu (O poezji Anny Kamienskiej). *Tygodnik Powszechny, 40*(24), 1, 5.

Szczypiorski, A. (1989). *Z notatnika stanu wojennego*. Poznan: SAWW. (Original work published 1984)

Tannen, D. (1979). What's in a frame? In R. O. Freedle (Ed.), *New directions in discourse processing* (pp. 137-181). Norwood, NJ: Ablex.

Tannen, D. (1985). Silence: Anything but. In D. Tannen & M. Saville-Troike (Eds.), *Perspectives on silence* (pp. 93-111). Norwood, NJ: Ablex.

Tannen, D. (1986). *That's not what I meant: How conversational style makes or breaks your realtions with others.* London: J. M. Dent & Sons.

Tannen, D. (1987). Repetition in conversation: Toward a poetics of talk. *Language, 63*(3) 574-605.

Tannen, D. (1990). Silence as conflict management in fiction and drama: Pinter's *Betrayal* and a short story, "Great Wits." In A. Grimshaw (Ed.), *Conflict talk* (pp. 260-279). Cambridge, UK: Cambridge University Press.

Tannen, D, & Öztek, P. C. (1981). Health to our mouth: Formulaic expressions in Turkish and Greek. In F. Coulmas (Ed.), *Conversational routine: Explorations in standardized communication situations and prepatterned speech* (pp. 37-54). The Hague: Mouton.

Tannen, D., & Saville-Troike, M. (Eds). (1985). *Perspectives on silence.* Norwood, NJ: Ablex.

The Second Foundation. (1981). Silence is deadly. In W. Gutwinski & G. Jolly (Eds.), *The Eighth LACUS Forum* (pp. 350-358). Columbia, SC: Hornbeam Press.

Thomas, J. A. (1983). Cross-cultural pragmatic failure. *Applied Linguistics, 4*(2), 91-112.

Tomkins, C. (1968). *The bridge and the bachelors: Five masters of the avant-garde.* New York: Viking.

Tyler, S. A. (1978). *The said and unsaid: Mind, meaning and culture.* New York: Academic Press.

Ure, J. (in press). "Letting-in devices" in the socialisation of new speakers: Cognitive development and the development of literary awareness in first and second language speakers. *Parlance,* 1-31.

Verschueren, J. (1985). *What people say they do with words: Prolegomena to an empirical-conceptual approach to linguistic action.* Norwood, NJ: Ablex.

Vestergaard, T., & Schroder, K. (1985). *The language of advertising.* Oxford, UK: Basil Blackwell.

Vikner, C. (1989). On linguistics and feeling insecure. In M. Herslund (Ed.), *Linguistic data and linguistic theory: Three essays on linguistic methodology* (Copenhagen Studies in Language 12; pp. 11-19). Copenhagen: Handelshojskoles Forlag.

Walker, A. G. (1985). The two faces of silence: The effect of witness hesitancy on lawyers' impressions. In D. Tannen & M. Saville-Troike (Eds.), *Perspectives on silence* (pp. 55-75). Norwood, NJ: Ablex.

Walkerdine, V. (1985). On the regulation of speaking and silence: Subjectivity, class and gender in contemporary schooling. In V. Walkerdine, C. Urwin, & C. Steedman (Eds.), *Language, gender and childhood* (pp. 203-241). London: Routlege & Kegan Paul.

Wardhaugh, R. (1985). *How conversation works.* Oxford, UK: Basil Blackwell.

Wardhaugh, R. (1986). *An introduction to sociolinguistics.* Oxford, UK: Basil Blackwell.

Watts, J. (1988, April 17). The great divide. *Observer,* pp. 33-34.

Wawak, J. (1989, August 8). Tablice nie wystarcza [The boards are not enough]. *Gazeta Wyborcza*, (65), p. 4.

Webster's Ninth New Collegiate Dictionary. (1983). Springfield, MA: Merriam-Webster.

West, C., & Zimmerman, D. H. (1983). Small insults: A study of interruptions in cross-sex conversations between unacquainted persons. In B. Thorne, C. Kramarae, & N. Henley (Eds.), *Language, gender, and society* (pp. 103-117). Rowley, MA: Newbury House.

Wolfson, N. (1981). Invitations, compliments and the competence of the native speaker. *International Journal of Psycholinguistics, 8*, 7-22.

Wolfson, N., Reisner, L. D'A., & Huber, L. (1983). The analysis of invitations in American English. In N. Wolfson & E. Judd (Eds.), *Sociolinguistics and language acquisition* (pp. 116-128). Rowley, MA: Newbury House.

Wooley, D. E. (1977). Iconic aspects of language. In R. di Pietro & E. L. Blansitt, Jr. (Eds.), *The Third LACUS Forum, 1976*. Columbia, SC: Hornbeam Press.

Zimmerman, D. H., & West, C. (1975). Sex roles, interruptions and silences in conversation. In B. Thorne & N. Henley (Eds.), *Language and sex: Difference and dominance* (pp. 105-129). Rowley, MA: Newbury House.

Zuengler, J. (1985). English, Swahili, or other languages? The relationship of educational development goals to language instruction in Kenya and Tanzania. In N. Nessa & J. Manes (Eds.), *Language of inequality* (pp. 241-254). Berlin: Mouton.

Index

Aborigines, 65n15
Advertising, 100-105
  irrelevance in, 100-103
  pseudocommunication in, 100
  repetition in, 104-105
Amare, Girma, 112-114
Ambivalence of silence, 66-69
Amish, 23-24
Amundsen, K., 128-129
Anger, 49
Anxiety, silence and, 21
Apache, 24, 53-54, 62
Argentina, 134-135
Aristotle, 125
Art, *See also* Painting
  repetition in, 104-105
  silence in Western, 141-144

Barundi, 109-110
Bateson, G., 147
Bauman, R., 39-42, 45-46
Beattie, G., 13
Belsey, C., 126-127
Black children, 20-21
Bradbury, R.J., 13
Brevity, 2
Brownmiller, S., 127
Buddhism, 142, 152
Burroughs, William, 161

Cage, John, 27n14, 143, 161-162
Cameron, D., 128
Carter, Jimmy, 106-108
Censorship, *See also* Self-censorship
  double-talk as, 117-118
  Eastern Europe, 110
  Poland, 130-131
Chafe, W.L., 13-14
Classification of silence, 167-168
Classroom, silence in, 10-11
  context and, 20-22
  foreign-language learning, 52-53
Codability, hesitation and, 14
Cognitive communication, 88-89
Communication, silence as, 3-4, 18, 70-71, *See also* Politics of silence; Relevance of silence
  absence of speech versus absence of sound, 71
  generalizations, 78-80
  Polish verb *milczec*, 71-78
  sociopragmatic basis, 34-35
  Western bias against, 45-48
Communicative intention, 84-89
Complaints, 49
Concrete poetry, 162
Context,
  in advertising, 101
  cross-cultural differences, 20-24
  relevance and, 90-93
Conversation,
  repetition in, 51
  style, 2
  temporal structure in, 88-89

Cool medium, 140-141, 160
Criminals, 124
Crown, C.L., 14-15
Cultural aspects of silence,
  cultural specificity, 22-23
  stereotpyes, 43-48
Cuna Indians, 62

Dauenhauer, B.P., 32-33
Definitions, linguistic, 30-32
Desaparecidos ("missing people"), 134-135
Dictatorships, 115
Directness, 2
Dortch, Richard, 111
Double-talk, 118
Duez, D., 15

Enninger, W., 23-24
Essentialism, 30-34
Ethnographic approach, 17-20, 70
Euphemisms, 114-115

Face-to-face interaction, silence in, 8-10
Faux pas, reactions to, 59-60
Feldstein, S., 14-15
Feminism, 120-121
Fibichner, 143-144
Fillmore, C.J., 58-59
Finland, 54
Formulaic silence, 59-62, 93, 167-168
4'33" (John Cage), 161-162
Frame analysis, 144-158
  applied to Edward Hopper, 149-151
  Japanese art, 151-153
  monochrome painting, 153-159
  of painting, 147-149
  types of silence and, 145-147
Framing, 19

Ganguly, S.N., 33-34
Gender, 44, 119, 138n4
Gilmore, P., 21
Gomringer, Eugen, 162
Graduation ceremony, 58

Hafif, M., 159
Hamlet (William Shakespeare), 145
Hart, Gary, 138-139n6
Hassan, I., 163
Hesitations, *See* Pausing
Hopper, Edward, 149-151
Hot medium, 140-141

Individual status, silence and, 135-136
Informative intention, 84-89
Interrupting, 119, 138n4
Invitations, responses to, 92-93
Involvement, 2
Italians, 55

Jakes, Milos, 133
Janway, Cecil, 110-111
Japanese,
  ambivalence of silence among, 67-68
  art, 151-153
  foreign-language classrooms, 52
  literature, 96-97n1
Johnson, M., 81-82, 146
Joking, 3-5
Judeo-Christian tradition, 125-126

Kamienska, Anna, 161
Kandinsky, Wassily, 153-154
Klein, Yves, 156-157, 165n5
Koppel, Ted, 111-114
Kuspit, D., 159

Lakoff, G., 81-82, 146
Language acquisition, 26n3
Leach, E.R., 39-40, 122-124, 137
Leave-takings, 49
Letting-in devices, 26n3
Literature,
  Japanese, 96-97n1

silence in, 24, 161-163
women writers, 121-122

McGuire, P.C., 94-95
Machine, human being as, 46
McLuhan, Marshall, 140-141
Malagasy, 44-45
Male silence, 5
Mallarmé, Stéphane, 161
Maltz, D.N., 36-46
Marcos, Ferdinand, 116
Martial law, 116
Mass media, 115-116
Mazowiecki, Tadeusz, 6-7
Meaninglessness, artistic, 142
Meditation, 18-19
Metaphors of silence, 81-84
theater and mime, 146-147
A Midsummer Night's Dream (William Shakespeare), 94-95
Milczec (Polish verb), 71-78
Mimes, 146
Miscommunication, 1-2, 4-5, 22-23
Monochrome painting, 153-159
Murray, S.O., 138n4
Music, silence in, 27n14, 142-143

Nail-biting, 58
Native Americans, 21-22, *See also specific tribes*
Navajo, 22
Negative functions of silence, 47-48, 66-69, 137
New Zealanders, 54
"Nightline" (television program), 111-114, 117
Nixon, Richard M., 114-115
Noise, silence versus, 37-43
Nonpropositional silences, 89-90
Northern Europeans, 54-55

Obituaries, 61-62
Oppressive silence, 115-118
application to groups, 122-125
in Poland, 129-131, 133-134
women and, 118-122, 125-129
Opting-out choice, 49
Ostensive-inferential communication, 84-85, 90

Painting, 143-144
frame analysis applied to, 147-151
linguistic silence and, 158-160
monochrome painting, 153-159
Pausing, 6-7, 51
classification of pauses, 13
in classroom, 10
psycholinguistics approaches to, 13-16
structuring of pauses, 88-89
at turn-taking junctures, 16-17
Penelope, J.S., 121-122
Pentecostals, 36, 38-40
Phatic communication, *See* Small talk
Philips, S.U., 18, 26-27n9
Poetry, silence in, 161-162
Poland, 116-117, 129-131, 133-134
Policemen, 124
Polish language, 71
Politeness, 2
Politics of silence, 98-137
absence of speech, 99
advertising, 100-105
Argentina, 134-135
individuals, 135-136
irrelevant words, 99
oppressive silence, 115-118
pausing, 6-7, 15
Poland, 129-131, 133-134
przemilczenie, 108-115
Rose Garden strategy, 107-106
status of oppressed, 122-125
strategic silence, 105-107
Tiananmen Square, 132-133
women's silence, 118-122, 125-129
Positive value of silence, 7-12
in classroom, 10-11
face-to-face interactions, 8-10
Propaganda, 104, 132
Prosody, 13

Przemilczenie ("not speaking about something"), 108-115, 130
Psycholinguistics, 13-16

Quakers, 36, 38-42, 45-46

Rank, 60-61
Rape, 127
Rauschenberg, Robert, 157-158
Rejection of invitation or offer, 52
Relevance of silence, 84-95
  advertising, 100-103
  art versus linguistics, 159-160
  example, 94-95
  informative intention and communicative intention, 84-90
  principle of relevance, 90-93
Religious worship, silence in, 36-48
  cultural stereotypes, 43-48
  noise versus silence, 37-43
Repetition, 51
  artistic exploitation of, 104-105
  in political propaganda, 104
Rhetorical questions, 35
Rock gardens, Japanese, 151-152
Rose Garden strategy, 107-106
Rothko, Mark, 165n4
Routine communication, 56-58
Rowe, M.B., 10-11
Ryman, Robert, 159

St. Paul, 119
Sapir, E., 64n5
Scandinavia, 54-55
Scenes from a Marriage (film), 52
Scientific language, 47
Scollon, R., 8-10, 41, 46
Scollon, S., 8-10
Self-censorship, 110-115
Semiotic approaches, 69-70
Shakespeare, William, 94-95, 145
Situational specificity, 22
Sleep (film), 104-105
Small talk, 53-62
Soap operas, 15
Soviet Union, 110
Spatial conceptualizations of silence, 82-84
Speech, silence versus,
  complementariness, 44-45, 48
  maintenance of open channel of communication, 48-53
  Polish verb *milczec*, 71-78
  religious worship, 37-38
  research guidelines, 79
  small talk, 53-62
  theoretical approaches, 12-13
Spender, D., 120
Sperber, D., 84-88, 90-92, 94, 99
Spitting, 57-58
Steiner, G., 141-143
Strategic silence, 105-108
Strong communication, 84
Subsequent version, 52
Swaggart, Jimmy, 110-111

Taboos,
  bodily functions, 137
  oppressed groups, 122-125
  political taboos, 110
  reactions to, 57-61
Tannen, D., 2, 67
Taoism, 142
Taxonomy of silence, impossibility of, 33
Television, pauses in, 15-16
Theatrical performances, 146
Theories, 31
Tiananmen Square, 132-133
Trappist monks, 26n6
Tygodnik Solidarnosc, 130-131

Unsaid, 44-45
Ure, J., 26n3

Vermeer, Jan, 144

Verschueren, J., 80-81

Walesa, Lech, 6-7
Warhol, Andy, 104-105
Warm Springs Indians, 55
Watts, J., 120
Weak communication, 84
Western view of silence,
  in artistic tradition, 141-144
  pausing, 6, 14-15
  small talk, 53-54
  tolerance of silence, 46
  women and, 128
Wieczór Wroclawia, 130
Wilson, D., 84-88, 90-92, 94, 99
Wolfe, S.J., 121-122
Women's abuse, 118-122, 125-129
Woolf, Virginia, 121

Zen Buddhism, 152

About the Author

Adam Jaworski, Ph. D., Poznan, has taught at the Department of English, Adam Mickiewicz University, Poznan, as well as at the University of Florida, Gainesville; The American University, Washington, DC; Birkbeck College, University of London, and is now Lecturer in Sociolinguistics at the Centre for Applied English Studies, University of Wales College of Cardiff.